2000
be at the heart of the
MiLLENNiUM

Leicester Mercury

Leicester Mercury
125

Leicester
Moments in Time

Leicester Mercury

Leicester Mercury 125

Leicester
Moments in Time

Breedon Books
Publishing Company
Derby

First published in Great Britain by
The Breedon Books Publishing Company Limited
Breedon House, 44 Friar Gate, Derby, DE1 1DA.
1998

ISBN 1 85983 137 0

Printed and bound by Butler & Tanner Ltd., Selwood Printing Works, Caxton
Road, Frome, Somerset.

Colour separations by Freelance Repro, Leicester.

Jackets printed by Lawrence-Allen, Avon.

Contents

Foreword

"Moments in Time." What an excellent title for a really first-class book.

Through its pages of carefully selected words and pictures, Leicestershire's famous past is proudly chronicled and its many special 'moments in time' well captured and recorded.

Historians tell us Leicester was founded by the Romans in 43AD. Records from that 'moment in time' are somewhat sketchy, as, sadly, it took another 19 centuries before the *Leicester Mercury* first hit the streets.

So, today, nearly 2,000 years later, the *Leicester Mercury* is proudly celebrating its 125th birthday on the eve of a new millennium.

Another really exciting period, with space-age technology, global markets and communication superhighways, all changing and shaping the way in which we all work and play.

Having been born in an era where my first experience of transportation systems was a hoop and stick, today's space-age travel and instant worldwide communication networks are difficult to comprehend.

Having also witnessed first hand, the sad demise of the 'ten bob' note, the wireless and the Ovaltinies (all very big in my Yorkshire youth) and seeing the rise of the Ecu, digital television and the Spice Girls, change, it could be argued, is not always for the better.

So back to the book. It is a tribute to past memories – some happy, some sad, but isn't that a reflection on life itself?

I trust you will get as much enjoyment from reading the book as I did in watching it being put together. It has been a labour of love and I sincerely hope it provides you with many more happy 'moments in time'.

Tony Hill OBE
Managing Director,
Leicester Mercury
August 1998

Introduction

Our first two books in this series captured scenes from Leicester's past in a collection of evocative photographs from the archives of the *Mercury*. This volume is an altogether more ambitious trip down memory lane – trying to capture the spirit of the century.

And what better way to view the past 100 years than through the cameras of *Mercury* photographers and the words of *Mercury* readers – a tremendous double act that has brought to life some of the extraordinary events of those changing times,

Once again we must thank Peter Hollins for all his hard work with the images and also Alex Dawson for the interviews.

Together they have given us a fascinating, sometimes moving but always interesting chronicle of times gone by. We hope you enjoy these *Moments in Time.*

Nick Carter
Editor-in-Chief
Leicester Mercury.

Old Leicester

The popular heart of Leicester, the Clock Tower. When laid down it was the most complex tramway junction in the country; indeed, the spot, with five main roads crossing, was always a bottleneck, even in mediaeval times. Before the idea for the Clock Tower, suggestions included a fountain, an illuminated clock, a statue to one of many local benefactors – and even a public urinal!

A glimpse of the Victorian citizenry, obligingly posing for the cameraman at the corner of Eastgate and New Bond Street. Note the sides of bacon and the hams dangling temptingly outside Johnson's provisions store.

Old Rutland Street about the time of World War One.

Huntingdon's Tower in High Street. Mary Queen of Scots, James I and also Charles I, on the eve of the Civil War, stayed there at one time or another. It was demolished in 1902.

Castle Street and Bath Lane at the turn of the century – the Mitre and Keys public house is just visible in the background.

The Clock Tower, pictured in 1904, showing one of the city's first electric trams.

Hoyel Street, looking towards St Martin's in the early 1920s. The lady appears to be waiting for the motorcycle rider to return.

Belgrave Gate in 1923 with electric trams, a bus, a cyclist and a horse and cart.

High Street at Carts Lane corner about 1905.

St Mary's Church early this century. A local gentleman takes a stroll along by the water.

The Reading Rooms on the corner of Granby Street and Belvoir Street between the wars.

A very wet and dreary day in Leicester looking from Rutland Street up towards Belvoir Street which crosses Granby Street, some time in the 1930s.

Memories ...Harry Limbert

DOWN Martin Street, Leicester, on a cold, wet Monday morning, went a small boy carrying a parcel.

He was heading for Palfreman's Pawn Shop, and in the parcel were his Sunday best clothes which his mother, following behind, was going to pledge until the next weekend.

Young Harry Limbert in sailor suit at a photographer's studio in Leicester, around 1922.

The regular Monday pawn shop visit is one of the earliest memories of 80-year-old Harry Limbert.

"Charlie, the manager, would open the shop at 7.30am on Monday mornings," says Harry. "And even at that time of the day there would be a queue waiting for him."

Martin Street, on the edge of Belgrave, was considered one of the roughest streets in Leicester in the 1930s.

"There were ten of us at number 180 Martin Street," says Harry. "Dad was a boot and shoe worker, but more out of work than in.

"I slept in a bed with two of my older brothers. In the summer they put me in the middle, and I couldn't get my breath. In the winter, they put me on the outside, where it wasn't as warm.

"There was one tap in the middle of the yard for six houses. When that froze, you used to light paper underneath it, to get it going again and get a kettle of water in the morning."

People on Martin Street were woken at 7.25am by buzzers on the three local engineering works. They were to remind workers that it was five minutes to go to clocking on time.

By nine, the delivery men were arriving – the Co-op milkman with milk at twopence-halfpenny a pint, and the Co-op baker with bread and cakes.

"Both delivered by horse and van," says Harry. "And they were paid by metal checks previously bought from any Co-op shop. No ordinary money changed hands with the vanmen."

By now almost all of Martin Street's many shops would be open. They ranged from a hat shop to a slaughterhouse; from an off-licence, to a bookmaker's runner, who took bets at the back door.

"But a favourite was the Tripe

Now retired, Harry Limbert teaches local children some of the old playground favourites.

Shop," says Mr Martin. "It only opened on Friday night, Saturday and Sunday mornings, for the sale of tripe and cow heel.

"You used to collect it in a billycan with the cup for a lid, because the lady in the shop used to fill the can with the liquor that the tripe was cooked in."

After school the children would play in the street – Hopping Nudge or Weak Horses or Marbles – often in the light of the gas lamps.

The street was quite safe, because a tollgate at one end deterred most vehicles from travelling down it.

And then it was bedtime, and the only noise was the odd row at the Martin Inn, and the midnight rumble of the *Flying Scotsman* on the nearby LNER line.

But 70 years and more have passed since then.

The *Flying Scotsman* has disappeared from Leicester. So has Palfreman's Pawn Shop, outside taps, horses and carts, bookmaker's runners and tripe shops. And so has Martin Street.

The tollgate and the railway bridge at the end of Martin Street.

The corner of Humberstone Gate and Rutland Street, possibly 70 or 80 years ago. This point, where the roadway narrows to normal width, was where the Humberstone Gate Fair used to end. It stretched from the weighbridge to the Clock Tower and round into Gallowtree Gate. This picture shows a farm produce auction in the New Hay Market section of Humberstone Gate.

Southgate Street near Peacock Lane in 1922. The scene could be many years earlier, however.

A young girl poses at the New Walk and Museum about 1900.

A peaceful day in King Street in the early part of this century. The house on the extreme left was the Edinburgh Hotel and later Waddington's Temperance Hotel.

Our picture shows a view of Stoneygate not long after the electric tramway system was opened in 1904. Note the ornate posts in the middle of the road from which were suspended the wires which carried the electric current.

The Clock Tower about 1905. Trams come and go but everyone feels free to stroll down the road.

Granby Street in the early part of the 20th century. Now the handcart seems a popular way to move goods.

Charles Street before redevelopment in the late 1920s.

A very quiet Charles Street in the late 1920s, looking in the opposite direction to the previous picture. Soon this view would all change as a modern street would rise up to replace this rundown area.

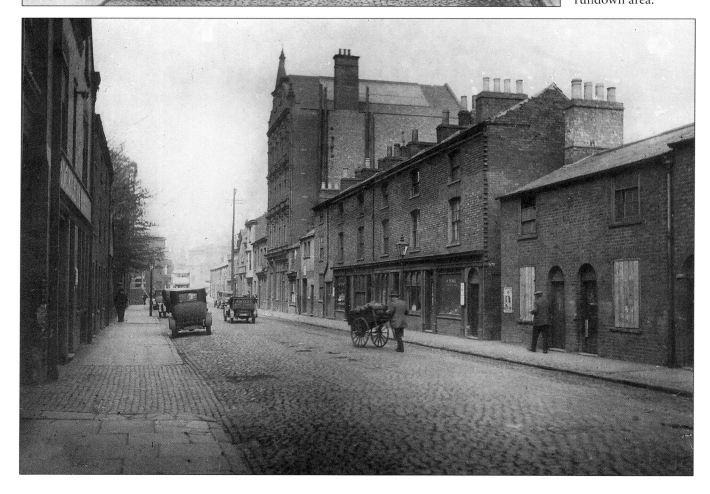

Bishop Street Post Office, c.1935. One van is advertising Rapid Firelighters.

Bishop Street Library in the 1930s.

Granby Street in late 1920s with the Post Office on the left.

Leicester's Town Hall in January 1938. A lone white-helmeted policeman stands outside the main entrance.

Stretton's factory in St Mary's Street in the 1930s.

St Martin's pictured in the 1930s. Grey Friars is to the right.

A new pedestrian crossing nearing completion on Gallowtree Gate on 12 May 1938.

Leicester Head Post Office on Granby Street, built in 1885 and demolished in 1935.

The Library on Belvoir Street and Wellington Street, pictured in October 1935.

The windows of Chantry House in The Newarke, which have looked out blindly since the time they were shattered by a bomb blast, are here being fitted with new stone window frames, in May 1953.

The Assembly Rooms in the 1930s, now called the City Rooms.

The Granby Halls in 1935. The advertisement tells of a 'Physical Culture and Athletics Institute' which offered such diverse pursuits as first-aid, gymnastics and folk dancing.

One of the chapels and crematorium at Gilroes Cemetery in Leicester in the 1930s.

How many people will recall this scene? The area now forms the St Margaret's Bus Station, in Burleys Way. At the time our picture was taken gas street lamps were still much in evidence.

Aylestone Road Methodist Church, put up for sale in November 1953 and purchased by Snushalls for use as a repository, has since been demolished.

Pictured in February 1960, the Haymarket Weighbridge, better known as the Humberstone Gate Weighbridge. When it first housed a public weighing machine in the early 1890s, the building then dominated The Haymarket.

The Midland Bank on Bishop Street in March 1960.

The beautifully ornate Turkey Cafe above Winns Cafe, seen here in February 1963.

The Crescent: Georgian terraced housing which are now business offices.

New Street in March 1955, looking towards Leicester Cathedral.

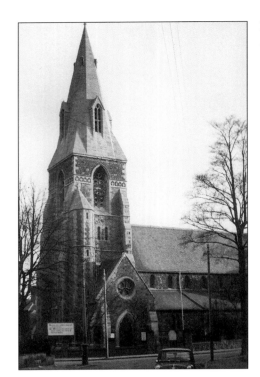

Now you see it, now you don't. St Peter's, Highfields, Leicester, on Sunday, 17 March 1968.

St Peter's on Sunday, 9 March 1969, after demolition of the steeple.

De Montfort Hall, Leicester, 11 May 1958.

The Clock Tower on the East Midland Gas Board's Aylestone Road premises, pictured on Sunday, 5 March 1967. It was erected in 1878.

Castle Gate House, Leicester, Saturday, 6 August 1966.

Wharf Street in the 1950s. Demolition has already taken place in some areas.

The Leicestershire Horse Repository in Charles Street in February 1959.

Cityscape

The demolition of the Stag and Pheasant Hotel on Humberstone Gate on 6 July 1961, looking towards the Clock Tower area. This is now the site of the Haymarket Centre.

London Road Station in September 1963, photographed from the roof of the *Evening Mail* offices showing the completed road widening scheme.

A view of Belgrave Gate in June 1961. Where the Leicester Palace once stood is the modern block of shops erected by Sketchley Ltd. The projection in the foreground was one of the new street lights.

Waterloo Street seen here in October 1962. All this area was demolished to make way for a new four-lane dual carriageway, now called Waterloo Way.

Upperton Road leading on to Narborough Road in February 1961.

In February 1956, the Roundabout, proposed for the junction of London Road and Mayfield Road, was calculated to slow down traffic and obviate jams like that shown here. When this picture was taken everything was at a standstill.

Hinckley Road in September 1963.

A scene in 1946 at Melton Road and Loughborough Road junction. A Trent Daimler double-decker bus, still with wartime white mudguards, pulls up as workmen construct a small traffic island.

London Road Railway Station and the Shell-BP House, seen here in May 1955.

A tree-lined Narborough Road in July 1955. Notice the rag and bone man's horse and cart.

Belvoir Street and Market Street in August 1955. To the right is Joseph Johnson's with Barnett's opposite.

In July 1950, a half-mile jam caused by road works to traffic islands and faulty traffic lights stretched from Victoria Park to the city centre.

August 1950 and the junction of Granby Street and Charles Street during resurfacing work. The van on the right is a Commer followed by an MG saloon. A Hillman Minx travels in the opposite direction.

Looking down on Gallowtree Gate in September 1958. The absence of parked cars resulted from a warning from the then Chief Constable.

A quiet High Street pictured in March 1956.

In August 1954, during reconstruction work in Belgrave Road, workmen brought to light a reminder of the tram days. It was along these lines, shortly after 4pm on 9 November 1949, that Leicester's last tram trundled its way to the depot. The rails were taken up but, defiantly, some metal remained in the ground.

Springtime in Town Hall Square, Leicester, in April 1959. The man bears an uncanny resemblance to Sir John Betjeman.

April 1960 – Traffic lights being installed to ease another bottleneck, the junction of St Nicholas Street and Great Central Street.

A World War Two photograph of Charles Street with Halford Street. The concrete box in the middle of the street was to hold water, for use by the National Fire Service. If the main water supply was hit by bombing they could use these man-made reservoirs.

Charles Street in November 1951. The car park became the Alliance and Leicester offices.

Memories… Konrad Smigielski

Leicester planning officer Konrad Smigielski (left) discusses the Market Place redevelopment scheme with consultant surveyor Mr J. D. Trustram Eve, in 1963.

Vision of the Future. Charles Street, Leicester, as it might have looked with the Smigielski monorail plan.

HE vowed he would never return to Leicester. The direct-speaking and passionate Konrad Smigielski said he had given the city his heart – and left with his heart broken.

"My tempestuous love affair with Leicester has come to an end," Mr Smigielski, the city's Chief Planning Officer, told the *Leicester Mercury* in May, 1972.

A dispute with councillors over the Sun Alliance building on Horsefair Street (he wanted it kept, and succeeded) meant Mr Smigielski left abruptly and unhappily after ten years in the top job.

He had initiated a series of sweeping changes to the city which even he admitted left it looking, temporarily, a little blitzed.

But it was Leicester's reluctance to follow him into the city of the future that really frustrated the passionate Pole.

His personal bird's eye view of Leicester was always of a space age city of urban motorways, extensive pedestrianisation with moving pavements and an innovative monorail from Beaumont Leys to Wigston to keep traffic out of the city centre.

"These changes I planned for Leicester – I did not expect them to happen overnight. But Leicester said my plans were science fiction – although they were carried out in Japan, America and Europe."

So he left Leicester, left town planning, and said he wasn't coming back to either. Ever.

"It was so frustrating," he said. "Nothing positive is being done in town planning or in anything else in Britain. So my plans which were seen in Leicester as surrealistic had to become reality elsewhere."

That monorail, for example. "I have seen a wonderful monorail system in Seattle, and it was beautiful – exactly what I wanted for Beaumont Leys."

But more than 20 years later, Konrad did return to Leicester.

It was really to publicise his novel *The Raphael Mystery*, a thriller based on Nazis purloining famous paintings during World War Two.

But he allowed himself to be shown round the centre of the city he had disowned with a heavy heart two decades before.

And he thought …it was actually pretty good.

In fact, it was a smiling Konrad who threw out his hands in joy on seeing the pedestrianised Gallowtree Gate.

"But this is marvellous," he cried. "It is just what I planned years ago. Thank you so much for bringing me here."

His eyes glistened too as he beheld the piazza of the Market Place which he had fought to keep, and he greeted the statue of the Duke of Rutland, which he had positioned, like an old friend.

He loved The Shires shopping centre too, particularly its Egyptian-style pillars.

The only thing he would not comment on was Leicester's traffic management system.

He admitted to some difficulty negotiating roads round the city he had known so well. "But I do not want to criticise, it would sound like sour grapes."

Yes, this visionary town planner thinks Leicester is moving in the right direction at last, as the millennium draws to a close. "But slowly. So slowly."

It turned out OK. Mr Smigielski takes in the Shires shopping centre in Leicester, on a recent return to the city.

Charles Street pictured in November 1951. This scene has changed many times since this photograph was taken. Now this area is a bus station.

Eric's Snack Bar site on Charles Street which, in October 1960, had been acquired for redevelopment.

1 March 1955 and traffic circles the Victoria Park Gates new island for the first time.

A June 1951 view of Charles Street, taken from the tower of Lewis's store in Humberstone Gate; beyond is Lee Street Circle, later to become Britain's first multi-storey car park.

The shape of things to come – a new traffic island at the junction of London Road and Evington Road was opened on 1 April 1955 for traffic to pass round it for the first time. The picture is taken looking towards Granville Road.

Work beginning on a new roundabout at the corner of Charles Street and Belgrave Gate in August 1952.

This Corporation-operated car park on the St George Street-Baker Street site – five minutes' walk from the Clock Tower – was never more than half-full during the day and the picture, taken from a nearby roof in November 1960, shows the extent to which it was used. This site became the *Leicester Mercury* offices in 1966.

A rather unlovely part of Navigation Street in October 1956. Burley's Flyover now straddles this area.

Gallowgate Gate in November 1964. This area is pedestrianised today.

Highcross Street at the junction of High Street in January 1961.

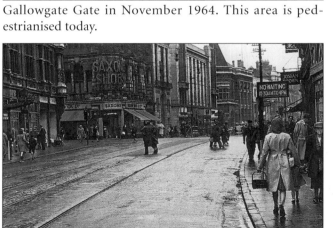

Granby Street on a cold, wet wintery day just after World War Two.

And a wet day in the 1950s looking down Granby Street.

A March 1958 view of London Road with East Street to the left. In the background is Northampton Square and the Police Headquarters.

Full to capacity, the East Street car park in November 1960, now the site of Leicester Law Courts.

Jarrom Street in April 1958. A bicycle is parked outside Plummers, the drapers.

A cold, wet King Richard's Road in December 1960.

Upper Conduit Street in May 1948. In the background is Sparkenhoe Street.

St Saviour's Road in February 1958.

Walnut Street in the early 1950s. Most of these buildings have now long gone.

Loseby Lane, a small but busy street, in late November 1958.

The policeman on point duty doesn't look too busy in London Road in April 1956.

A view from Northampton Square in March 1958. In the background is the YMCA and to the right is Harris of Granby Corner.

Newarke Street, August 1955, with excavators and pneumatic drills at work on repairing the road surface.

Burnmoor Street with Leicester City Football Club's main stand behind in August 1973. This stand has since been replaced.

Floodlights being erected at Leicester City's ground in August 1957. This view is from Filbert Street.

Air pollution isn't a new thing. What the Aylestone district looked like with the morning sun trying to pierce the gloom created by the smoke from thousands of house chimneys. The picture was taken from the roof of the Colleges of Art and Technology, looking towards the power station, in January 1954.

Next Please

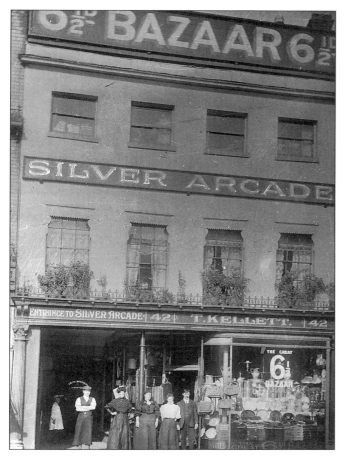

The Sixpence-halfpenny Bazaar in Silver Arcade as it appeared in 1908.

The premises of William Hallam, 'General Dealer' on the south-east corner of High Street and Highcross Street immediately before demolition about 1902.

Henry Clarke's new shop front on 1905 Pictured in the doorway are Henry Clarke senior and Nancy Clarke, sister of the present Henry Clarke, the business having been in the same family for three generations.

The shop at the junction of Carlton Street and Lower Brown Street housed the family butcher's business of Mr Frederick Ireland, who is pictured posing proudly in the shop doorway. The meat displayed in the window would no doubt trouble today's health inspectors.

This delightful view shows the Victoria Parade butcher's premises of Hardyman. Note the hams hanging up outside. This would not be allowed today. A notice offers for sale soups in glasses and tins.

The last fair on Ross's Walk in 1921. The boy in the photograph – Frank Rayns – was 12 years old then. The man is Jack Breakes and they were selling brandysnap at one old penny a bag.

Charles Draper's daughter, Mary Draper, with a warehouseman at 103 Belgrave Gate. The business was founded in 1903.

Who could resist buying something from this butcher's shop packed with goodies? The shop was in Oxford Street, Leicester, and the photograph was taken in 1912. And as you can see 6d went rather a long way in those days.

The premises of Mr William Hughes at the corner of Russell Square and Woodboy Street, Leicester, about 1926. Originally it was a general store run by his widowed mother. Mr Hughes took over the business in 1910 after he left the pawnbroking trade. He turned it into a men's outfitters and haberdashery. The shop was eventually (after the photograph was taken) enlarged to Nos 2, 4 and 6 Russell Square. Mr Hughes died in 1954.

This shop in Bowling Green Street, Leicester, helped provide Leicester Suffragettes with some of their fighting funds by selling books, posters and postcards to support the cause.

Atmospheric timepiece – rich in period detail, this picture of Bill Sampson's market stall was found by his niece, Miss Bessie Jones, of Knighton. It is probably from the early 1920s.

The Covent Garden Fruit Stall in Leicester Market in the 1920s.

The day's work begins, a driver has unloaded his goods and prepares to set off on his horse and cart while tradesmen and women start choosing stock for their customers at the wholesale fruit and vegetable market on Halford Street.

The village grocery, over 300 years old, as it was in the 1930s. In the picture with Mr and Mrs Moore is their niece, Nora, who became Walcote School headmistress. Mrs Moore, Somerset-born, moved to Walcote in 1919 as a Land Army girl and met her late husband Ernest in the village. Together they were an essential part of Walcote, Mr Moore delivering the post for 19 years.

Curry's Cycle Shop in Belgrave Gate, Leicester, in 1902. Now Curry's, a national electrical goods and TV merchandiser, has been taken over. But the history – the firm was founded in Leicester – remains.

Here we see a shop which belonged to W. Ward, the tobacconist, on the corner of The Newarke and Southgate Street during demolition in the 1930s.

Mrs Emma French had her corner shop at the junction of Macdonald Road and Ross Walk, Belgrave. She is pictured in the doorway with a young neighbour – Peter Bradshaw – in 1925. Her surviving daughter, Mrs Edna Neale, remembers filling 1lb and 2lb bags with sugar from half-hundredweight sacks when very young – no pre-packaging in those days.

Three shops in Regent Street, Hinckley, which were demolished to make way for new building society offices in March 1960.

Worthington's cash stores in Beatrice Road, Newfoundpool, pictured in 1930. Mr C. H. Ward, manager, is on the left. The prices make an interesting comparison with those of today. New-laid eggs were five for one shilling (5p) and Danish bacon was 1s 3d per pound (about 7½p in today's equivalent).

York's of 16 Wharf Street, purveyors of high-class confectionery, pictured in the 1920s. By 1936, Leicester, was the most prosperous city in the British Empire. But in Wharf Street families of five lived crammed into a single room. The area bounded by Belgrave Road to the west, Humberstone Road to the south and the Great Northern Railway, had the reputation of being the poorest and roughest in the city. Those who did not live there kept well away from it and legend had it that policemen only ventured there in pairs.

Vickers, Mount Grocers of Gallowtree Gate, c.1908. The photograph was submitted by Mr J. H. Meigh of Ilkeston, Derbyshire. His father worked at Vickers Mount, after working for Herricks at a branch at 272-4 Belgrave Gate. Mr Meigh was born in Martin Street and although his family moved to Grantham when he was a year old, they visited his grandparents in Burfield Street for years afterwards.

No 3 Narborough Road, a cycle shop, the premises of Leedham & Son since 1919. Before that time it was a fruiterer's.

In August 1955, Bill White was known as the 'lone shopkeeper of Brook Street', centre of the slum clearance area. He said, "I've not been offered alternative accommodation by the Corporation. They're trying to starve me out and after all I've done for the city you'd think they would help me now." Mr White said that as Pearly King he had collected between £16,000 and £17,000 for charity in Leicester and felt he was being shabbily treated. He had kept his little general store for about 30 years, but sales were dropping by £30 a week as families left the area when their homes were knocked down.

The Pembroke Street Post Office in November 1955. In the doorway are Mr and Mrs Ayres and with David.

'Charney', as the locals had come to know Charnwood Street, was Leicester's Portobello Road. It was demolished in the early 1970s. This picture was taken in October 1957.

F. W. Walker's grocery shop at 191 Charnwood Street, seen here in November 1961.

Granby Street in June 1958 with Knight's, men's outfitters, Ellis china shop and Rayner's, the opticians.

Granby Street-Belvoir Street corner in March 1959.

Boots' old frontage, Gallowtree Gate, in February 1959. Boots' cafe was on the first floor with waitress service available.

Granby Street in June 1958. The shops are Burbidge & Co and Browett's car showroom who sold Triumph and Standard cars.

Sale time! Some of the queue who waited through the night in the hope of getting radio and television bargains in December 1956.

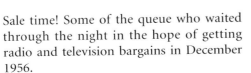

The Corridor, which extended from the Fish Market to F. W. Woolworth in Market Place, seen here in July 1961.

The style and flavour of Victorian architecture make Leicester's Silver Arcade one of the city's most interesting shopping areas. A face-lift in 1979 had restored the Arcade and created a suite of offices.

The March sunshine casts long shadows on these shoppers and schoolgirls as they make their way through Victoria Parade some time in the 1950s.

Winn's Oriental Cafe and Restaurant and Tom Browne men's outfitters in the Market Place in the 1950s.

At the top of Market Place stood Winn's Oriental Cafe & Restaurant as viewed here in September 1954, later becoming Woolworth's store. Other shops were Maples, Maypole and Liptons, etc.

The Mikado Cafe in the Market Place in April 1961.

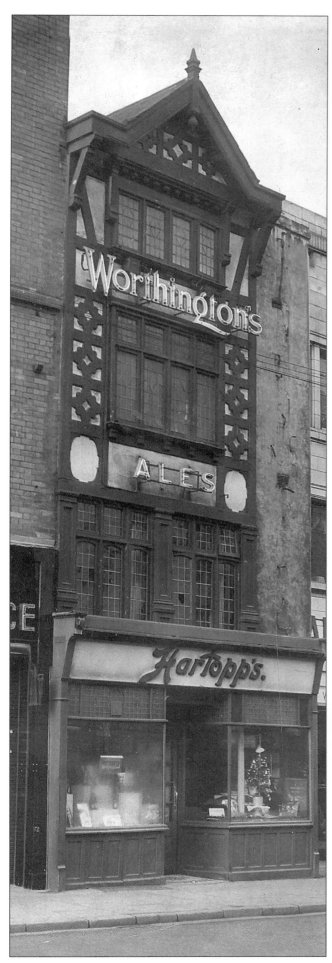

The Albion restaurant, Gallowtree Gate, which closed at the end of 1953.

An early evening view of Spalls in Gallowtree Gate in 1961. It was sold that year for £200,000.

This scene, pictured in February 1955, shows Eastgates, the Haymarket to the right and looking down Church Gate.

Looking down on the interior of the wholesale fruit and vegetable market on Halford Street as the day's produce is set out for the greengrocers' shops and market traders to take their pick.

Memories… The Lakhani Family

FROM the outside, it looks like an unassuming street-corner restaurant on Leicester's Asian-influenced 'Golden Mile'.

In fact it's an award winner, recommended as 'brilliant, fascinating and authentic' in the national *Good Food Guide*.

But it's the tale behind Bobby's restaurant that makes it even more special. It is the business built on a double disaster: Idi Amin, and near financial ruin.

Founder Mr Bhagwanji Lakhani and his wife Mangla are Ugandan Asians, expelled with their six children by the tyrant Amin in 1972.

About 40,000 Asians came to Britain after being thrown out by Amin. Around 6,000 settled in Leicester.

Mr Lakhani had been a highly successful businessman in Uganda, with an empire stretching from furniture and electrical workshops to dry cleaning.

And what's more he managed to get some of his money out of the country too – although businesses and three family houses were abandoned.

"We had 90 days to get out, so we left a lot behind in Uganda," says Mrs Lakhani. "Leicester was not completely strange to us. We had visited the city before, because two daughters were studying here."

But Mr Lakhani's initial British business ventures were disasters, through bad luck and bad advice.

"We had a factory making ice lollies," says son Dharmesh. "But in the first year that made a big loss – the lollies had not had preservatives in, and rotted. We lost £30,000 worth of stock."

Mr Lakhani suffered again with property investments. "We bought property that had been unoccupied for some time," said another son, Atul. "Not realising how quickly the British weather wears buildings away."

By 1975, Mr Lakhani's African money had evaporated like water in the dry season.

"I did not want to sign on," explains Mr Lakhani senior. "I told my wife we had lost the money, let's try something. We decided to try a restaurant and at last got lucky."

The decision might seem a curious one. The family had no restaurant experience whatsoever. In fact, Mr Lakhani had never even been into a restaurant, until he stood nervously in his own.

But with his wife as chief cook, Mr Lakhani as proprietor, family members rallying round and a second mortgage, the idea turned out to be inspired.

The vegetarian restaurant opened on St Valentine's Day, 1976, it's un-Asian name taken from a popular Indian film.

And you could say it is now internationally known. Atul Lakhani

Mr and Mrs Lakhani with head chef Kala Lakhani.

was in Bombay recently talking food with an enthusiastic technician from South Wales.

"There's a restaurant in Leicester I've heard a lot about," said the man. "It's not Bobby's is it?" asked Atul. "That's it!" said the man. "D'you know it?"

The Asian family from Africa now feel Leicester is very much their home.

"There's nothing for us in Africa now," said Mrs Lakhani. "And we are foreigners in India too. No, we're staying in Leicester." And she adds with a smile, "You don't think they'll throw us out again do you?"

What with all those brilliant recipes? Not a chance!

Picture are (left to right) Atul Lakhani, Bhagwanji Lakhani, Mangla Lakhani, Dharmesh Lakhani and Enna Lakhani.

Mr Syd Powell and his assistant, Miss Susan Oram, at their improvised fruit stall with parasol cover in Loughborough Market in October 1970.

Leicester Cattle Market in the 1960s.

Honest Toil

Better-British-Costs less

Leicester leads in Typewriters

The Imperial factory at North Evington is working at high pressure, finding employment for Leicester workers, and furnishing the world with better typewriters. Governments, public bodies, and many of the world's greatest businesses are using the Leicester-made Imperial.

Imperial

IMPERIAL TYPEWRITER CO. LTD.
Head Office and Works :
North Evington, LEICESTER
Telephone : 27174/5   Telegrams : "Typewriter, Leicester"

Leicester leads in typewriters. The Imperial factory at North Evington is working at high pressure finding employment for Leicester workers, and furnishing the world with better typewriters. Governments, public bodies, and many of the world's greatest businesses all used the Leicester-made Imperial, states this advertisement from 1932.

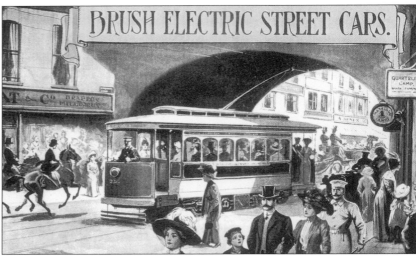

The front cover of the Brush Electrical Engineering Co catalogue of 1912. Inside were examples of electric street cars (tramcars) which were available for export worldwide.

Corset manufacturer R. W. & H. Symington was established at Market Harborough in 1856. During mid-Victorian times the firm developed from a cottage industry making 'stays' to the town's major employer, thanks to the emphasis on narrow waists in ladies' fashion. In 1884, corset manufacture was transferred to the large and ornate red brick factory in Adam and Eve Street. When this closed a century later, it housed 3,000 items of costume which were subsequently donated to Leicestershire Museums. The collection includes an inflatable bra from 1950s, an Edwardian corset specially designed for the tropics and a wide range of bust improvers.

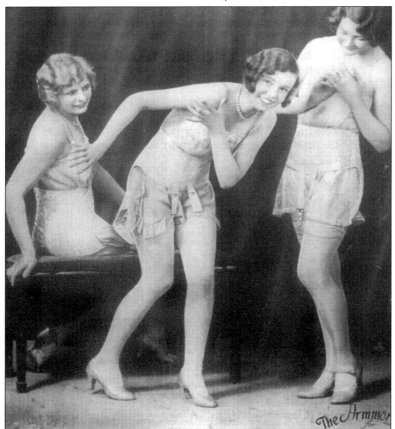

Fox's Glacier Mints company offices in June 1962. The Leicester wholesale grocery business of Joyce & Fox was extended to sweet manufacture in the 1890s, but in 1897 the partnership was dissolved. W. R. Fox continued to make sweets, and was joined in 1914 by his son, Eric, who had returned from studying business methods in America. In 1919, the firm registered the name Glacier, and the manufacturing business became known as Fox's Glacier Mints from 1925. Vigorous advertising during the early 1920s established the Glacier Mints nationally, along with the polar bear character. They are still going strong today.

The premises of Alex Laurence at 2-4 King Street, seen here at the turn of the century. The firm was the only piano manufacturer in Leicester, started in 1864.

At the boatyard. As well as the barges they made pontoons, punts, and all sorts of pleasure craft. The boy on the front of the photograph is holding a card which probably advertised the boat building business: Mr William Rudkin's grandfather, father and uncles at Rudkin's Boatyard near Syston Street.

This is how the milk used to be delivered to your door with a man pushing a handcart on which stood a large milk churn, He would then extract the exact amount you required. This is the late Sidney Hitchens, of the Co-op, in the 1920s.

Leicester Corporation Furnaces at the West Humberstone refuse destructor. The furnaces were kept going 24 hours a day, supplied steam and hot water to Spence Street Baths, and generated electric current for all work at the destructor.

This two-man team kept Birstall's streets clean with their handcart, brush and spades. Messrs Martin and Stewart are having a well-earned rest some time in the 1920s.

My old man's a dustman! Long before the days of wheelie bins, the 'centre gang' at work in Belvoir Street, Leicester. Left to right: Jock Bracey, Nobby Clarke, Chissah Brown, foreman Albert Pawley and Walter Chawner, in June 1968.

A street cleaner in the 1950s. Nowadays it's all mechanised but in those days you had to trudge round streets pushing your barrow and cleaning the pavements and gutters. This view is now the site of the Holiday Inn, St Nicholas Circle.

Leicester Water Department officials demonstrate a street standpipe in October 1959.

Nurses at the turn of the century in the Leicester Lunatic Asylum.

Bosworth Park Infirmary: On the left in the picture Enrolled Nurse M. March of Market Bosworth, right Pupil Nurse S. Parry of Nailstone, and to the rear Enrolled Nurse D. D. Smith of Shenton, in April 1966.

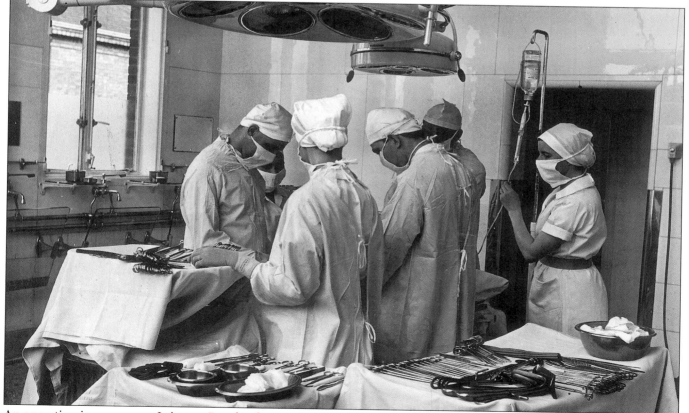

An operation in progress at Leicester Royal Infirmary in May 1966.

Postmen outside the village post office in 1919. Billesdon must have been an important centre for rural deliveries in those days.

A postman's lot is never an easy one. It's always hard on the feet but sometimes the weird way we address our letters makes it hard on the head too. Postman Alan Ackerley with a fist-full of problems in January 1975.

Leicester's tallest postman, Jack Flanagan, bends nearly double to negotiate a low letterbox, typical of many found on Leicester's newer private estates, in July 1962.

October 1960 and a striking picture of a huge pile of parcels being sorted, put into bags, and sent away. Over 12,000 parcels pass through the Campbell Street office every night.

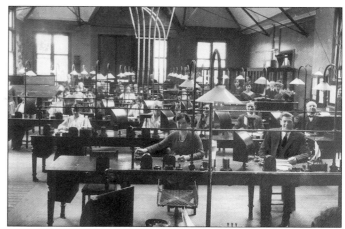

The old Telegraph Instrument room at the corner of Bishop Street and Granby Street which was on the first floor of the General Post Office before it moved to the present position further along Bishop Street. It shows the days of 'Morse only' for transmitting telegrams. Direct telegraph lines existed to London, Birmingham, Leeds, Manchester and Liverpool. Minor lines were connected to Market Harborough, Kettering, Bedford, Northampton, Melton Mowbray and Loughborough. A teleprinter system was introduced in the early 1930s.

F. Pollard's machine shop in 1938. 'Corona' Machine Tool Works, St Saviour's Road East.

The Leicester Telephone Exchange in Rutland Street with its all-female operators and supervisors. The picture was taken about 1912.

Mechanic Arthur Burton and knitter Raymond Merryfield make sure the cones keep turning on the circular machines at T. W. Kempton Ltd in October 1967.

Yvonne Spencer, a 15-year-old in her third week in the Corah training school in September 1969, receives instruction in tights elasticating from Mrs Dorothy Beck.

Cleaning in focus: Gerry Broughton's photograph of laundry service hand Ann Turner.

Jelson's own plant on site at Leicester Stadium in the 1930s.

Pictured in November 1959, changing view from the Upperton Road bridge, Leicester, where a 22-acre site was being developed by the timber firm of William Gimson & Sons. The site is bounded by the River Soar and the canal, the main Central Leicester-London railway line and the Midland Leicester to Burton line. This will be the site of Leicester City Football Club's new stadium in the next century.

Memories… Harry Smith

The Coal Strike Is Over declared the headline in the *Leicester Mercury*, back in March 1972.

And the story was illustrated with the foreboding 6ft 1in figure of Harry Smith, a miner at Snibston Colliery in Coalville.

Mr Smith was pictured as he left the pit and crossed Ashby Road for the short walk to the pit baths.

He had been one of the first miners back after the 51-day strike, called when the miners' demand for £28 per week were rejected by the National Coal Board.

Harry Smith at Snibston Pit in 1972, after finishing safety work to enable the pit to re-open.

Mr Smith had been carrying out Sunday safety work at Snibston, before coal production started again on Monday.

"I remember when they took that photograph," laughs Mr Smith. "We were allowed back in to clear up some girders, and make sure that the pit was safe."

For the average householder, the end of the 1972 strike also meant the end of rationed light and heat, interrupted television, and for some a three-day working week.

For Leicestershire miners like Mr Smith, the return to work meant the end of seven weeks without pay.

"It was tough," he recalls, "because not only was I on strike, but my wife was also on strike. She worked at Coleorton Hall.

"We had two children to bring up, and the money you got for picketing was nothing really. We had to dip into our savings."

The press were unimpressed by the strike.

But locally at least, people were much more sympathetic. Mr Smith remembers local teachers putting his two children on free school meals for the duration of the strike.

And at Filbert Street, collections for the miners were passed round before Leicester City matches.

Today Mr Smith says, "I don't really agree with strikes. But the 1972 strike was worth it. Not only was our pay improved, but more importantly, safety standards were improved. We went back to work much happier."

Mr Smith started in the mines in 1950, working at the pit bottom and at the coal face, with pick and shovel, and later with machinery.

"It was hard physical work, horrible work really when you think about it," he says. "We would be kneeling at a coal seam a metre high, for a seven-and-a-quarter hour shift, about 700 metres underground. I've seen people killed underground, and I've been injured myself.

"The average person today wouldn't believe the conditions we worked under. And the best wage when I started was £8 a week"

But the work bred a comradeship which held the men together, and at one time held the town of Coalville together too.

Today there is no mining left at all in Leicestershire, and Mr Smith believes Coalville is the poorer for it.

"We've just got the Snibston Museum now," he said. "That's the memorial to the pit.

"And when you see modern, highly-paid footballers exhausted when they have to play twice in a week, you wonder whether young lads would want a mining job anyway."

Harry re-visits the Snibston pit, now an industrial museum.

Demolition experts bring the first of two huge coal hoppers toppling to the ground at a now-closed Snibston pit, in 1986.

The Art Deco style frontage of Kirby & West Dairy which is now demolished.

A famous manufacturer in Leicester was Bentley Engineering, pictured here in June 1962.

The Dalma Works in Junior Street, Leicester, which was acquired by N. Corah (St Margaret) Ltd, in September 1960.

Murphy's offices in January 1954. This site later became The Metal Box Co Ltd.

Everard's Brewery, Castle Street, c.1937.

A view of the factory of Luke Turner & Co Ltd, in Jarrom Street. A large area off Jarrom Street had been cleared, in September 1958.

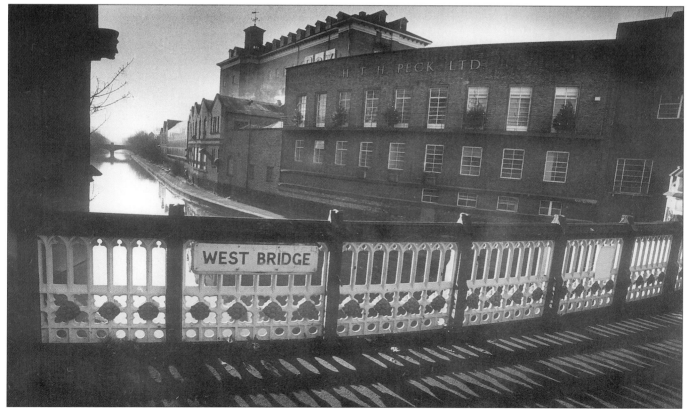

H. T. H. Peck Ltd, 'PEX' of West Bridge.

Mrs Jean Simmons crisp testing at Walker's Crisps in May 1972.

At Nabisco-Frears Biscuits, Mrs B. Howlett collects the fresh biscuits – just a few minutes old – and sends them on to the next stage of their journey, checking all the time for the occasional broken one, in March 1967.

In July 1952, Mr William Cartwright of Leicester Road, Wigston Magna has just completed 50 years in his trade but has no intention of retiring. He obviously enjoys his work, which he started on leaving school and helped his father, a sweep in the Wigstons for 37 years. In those days he received 3d or 4d per chimney.

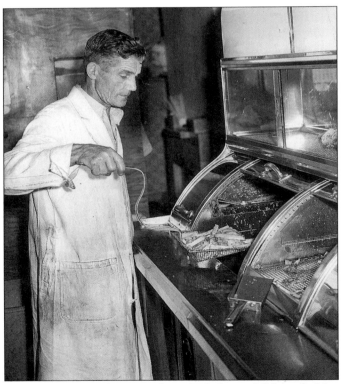

Chips fried to perfection. The British love of fish and chips goes on and on and things haven't altered much since this photograph of July 1960.

The days of steam rollers and road gangs such as this have long gone, but the pride that these workers had in their labours is still written on their faces for all to see.

This 1950s photograph of a miner at Whitwick Colliery, feeding a pit pony from his snap tin, brought world-wide acclaim for photographer Mr Don Ottey.

Yardmen with a shunting engine in Snibston pityard in the early 1900s.

The last miners in the North Leicestershire Coalfield came out of the darkness for the final time – and into the whiteness of blizzards. Mr Peter Sheath, centre, and his colleagues finished the last production shift at the record-breaking Bagworth Colliery. The pit's 165-year history came to an end as miners brought the last piece of coal to the surface in February 1991.

Pictured four days before Christmas 1961, the headstocks and colliery yard at Snibston. The steel cables for raising and lowering the cages pass over the wheels and into the winding house on the right.

Engineers making final tests at the tunnels which contain the 1,500lbs of explosives at Breedon Cloud Hill Quarry.

Holwell Works, Asfordby, just after World War Two.

May 1974 at East Midlands Airport saw a change in uniform with models showing the two new styles while Sindy Gill, in the centre, wears the old style. The most striking difference is the new bowler hats which were chosen by the air hostesses themselves.

The first of three British Aircraft Corporation 1-11 jet airliners became the property of British Midland Airways when, at a ceremony at the East Midlands Airport, the aircraft was officially handed over. Mr J. H. Hodgson, chairman of BMA, officially accepted the new 550mph Rolls-Royce powered jet, valued at about £1.5 million.

Dial 999!

This fire scene in Belvoir Street is thought to have been photographed in 1887. Note the absence of fire fighting equipment.

The opening of Rutland Street Fire Station in 1892. Firemen demonstrate equipment to the public. Note the magnificent brass helmets.

A turnout from the former Fire Station in Rutland Street late last century.

The Fire Engine Station in Bowling Green Street in 1892 with two horse-drawn appliances. Superintendent Ely is third from the left in the front row.

Horse-drawn escape, outside Asfordby Street Fire Station – the bay horse was called Charlie – in 1899.

Shepshed Fire Brigade in 1902. With buttons and helmets gleaming, they pose for a portrait on the occasion of the Coronation of King Edward VII.

You may be able to spot relatives on this old picture of Leicester City Fire Brigade taken at Asfordby Street in 1905. It has been kept by Mrs Phyllis Butcher of 79 Buxton Street. It was passed on to her by her father, Mr Frederick Ames, a member of the brigade who is in the picture, top row, far right.

Aftermath: This scene, so suggestive of the Leicester blitz which followed many years later, shows the total devastation wreaked on Rowley's factory by the great fire in Queen Street in 1911.

Firemen's drill: A scene about 1912 with firemen carrying out drill at the old Rutland Street Station. Notice the man on the left is wearing early breathing apparatus. The helmet is fed air by a fireman behind him with bellows attached to a long pipe.

Pictured at Rutland Street Fire Station in 1912, Leicester's first motorised fire appliance, made by Merryweather.

Many large companies today still have their own internal fire brigade. Our picture shows an unknown private company pictured in 1920 with a trophy they have evidently won in some fire-fighting competition.

Seen here in July 1943 is a National Fire Service fireboat. They were used during the war to tackle any canalside factories that were hit by bombing.

Five hundred people evacuated Marks and Spencer's, Gallowtree Gate, Leicester, store in 85 seconds when the fire alarm sounded as dense smoke was seen pouring from the roof in October 1967. Within three minutes four fire appliances were at the scene with firemen fighting the flames, rescuing three men trapped on the roof and searching for a 'missing' member of the staff. Fortunately it was all an exercise, part of the 'Keep Leicester Fire Safe' campaign.

One of the biggest fires in Leicester in recent years broke out in the top floors of the Belvoir Street furniture and carpet store of Waring & Gillow in October 1971.

A line of fire appliances stand empty outside the Infirmary in June 1974, their crews inside helping fight the blaze and evacuate patients as the smoke, less severe than when they first arrived, still belches from windows. Above the bridge the crew of the hydraulic platform continue their window-to-window search for anyone still trapped.

A 'Green Goddess' named Doris and her crew of servicemen getting a farewell wave from office workers as they left County Hall, Glenfield in January 1978. Their firefighting duty in Leicester finished after covering during the national firemen's strike.

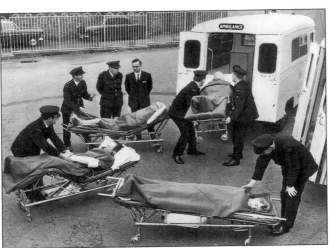

In September 1968, ambulances were fitted with removable trolley beds instead of the usual fixed bed bench and stretcher, which were becoming necessary with the increasing popularity of shopping precincts and tall blocks of flats. Leicester Ambulance Service was among the first in the country to be equipped with two such ambulance units, each consisting of two trolley beds which can be made rigid in the vehicle and also used as seats for sitting patients.

In addition to its fire fighting role, the Borough Brigade also provided a horse-drawn ambulance at the Central Fire Station, Rutland Street, Leicester. It was introduced in 1890 and used until 1921.

Leicester Police pictured in 1893 with Superintendent Ormiston (centre front).

Leicester Borough Police Band, pictured in 1900.

A smart line-up of police officers about to go on duty on their new mopeds, pictured around the late 1940s.

Leicestershire and Rutland County Constabulary Mobile Police Station built on an Austin 25cwt van chassis, seen here in February 1952. The kitchen could cater for 100 people if necessary. Cooking was done on petrol and gas stoves, all stores and equipment being carried in the special van. The vehicle was later used in the East Coast Floods relief.

Memories… Jock Joiner

The first traffic wardens, taking part in a Remembrance Day parade in 1961.

JOCK Joiner spent 30 years in Leicester's police force, from 1935 to 1965, mainly in the CID.

He investigated any number of robberies, rapes and murders, and was shot at twice ("They missed both times!").

But it's not for any of these he is likely to be remembered. And the tough Scot, now well into his 80s, won't tell you much about them anyway.

No, he may well be best remembered for something he did towards the end of his police career.

Jock Joiner at the time he joined Leicester police, in 1935.

Under the orders of the then Chief Constable Robert Mark, he introduced Britain's first proper traffic wardens to Leicester.

London had some wardens already – but they just kept watch on the meters.

The idea in Leicester was to have a city of properly controlled parking regulations, enforced by the wardens.

"The Chief Constable called me into his office early in 1961, to ask how the recruiting and training was going on," remembers Jock. "And he asked if the traffic wardens could be introduced on 13 March.

"And then he said, 'When I go to the Chief Officers' Conference, they're all going to ask me when we brought them in. My birthday's on 13 March, so I won't forget.'"

So on 13 March 1961, the first 12 traffic wardens – six male, six female – hit the streets of Leicester.

"They went out for the first fortnight with no fixed penalty tickets," says Mr Joiner.

"They just advised and warned. A softening-up process, and it worked wonders."

Traffic wardens did not only reinforce parking laws. They also freed police to spend more time preventing crime, and detecting criminals.

"People came from all over the country to examine our system," says Mr Joiner. "They were sometimes amazed at a line of traffic on one side of the road, with the other side completely traffic free."

Over the years, Jock collected virtually every illegal parking excuse there is. "There was even a parson who tried to tell me my traffic warden had got the wrong time on his ticket, because he remembered hearing the Leicester Clock Tower clock strike eleven. The Clock Tower clock doesn't strike the hour."

Mr Joiner says he reckons the biggest change in the police force generally is the decline of the bobby on the beat.

"You had your own patch when I started, and if anything happened on that patch, it was your responsibility.

"If a factory was broken into, and I hadn't noticed a tampered lock or something, the boss would want to know why. I've been hauled out of bed, ordered down to the police station, and given a right rollicking.

Jock Joiner today, at home in Anstey, Leicestershire.

"It was a hard life sometimes, very disciplined. And all on £3 2s 0d a week, plus £1 5s 0d housing allowance and 1s a week boot allowance."

And has he ever got a parking ticket himself? "Yes, I have, but I didn't curse the traffic warden. I had been in a hurry and hadn't noticed the restriction. It was my own fault."

A Police public call post and Police, Fire and Ambulance telephone in a Leicester street in September 1960.

Leicestershire detectives outside a bank in Narborough where a robbery took place in October 1962.

Police Constable John Tipler, of Broughton Astley, with a Mini-Moke on trial in December 1965.

Their own opinions of The Beatles commendably concealed behind good-natured grins, a line of policemen straining to hold back the surging youngsters in Charles Street in October 1963. The fans were queuing to buy tickets to the 'Fab Four's' concert.

A parade of 'Panda' cars at the force's new traffic headquarters at Enderby in April 1968. The 17 Pandas moved into action in four areas of Leicestershire and Rutland as Chief Constable Mr John A. Taylor launched the latest battle in his war on crime.

In the Coalville, Hinckley and Melton and Rutland divisions 'rural section beat policing' was begun, using the distinctive Morris 1000 cars with white vertical stripes down the blue bodywork.

Three-year-old Fenella Lewin temporarily parted from her mother while shopping in Leicester in April 1970, needed no further proof of the usefulness of policewomen than the comforting presence of PWC Delia Dunkley. The problems of children occupy only a part of the working life of women police.

Police officers board a Midland Red coach during the Miners' Strike in May 1972.

When PC James Mulligan asked the children of Newtown Linford village school, "Would you mind accompanying me?" they did not mind at all, for PC Mulligan was inviting them to take part in a conga around the school lawn to celebrate the end of a week he had spent with them. The children, together with the children of Swithland School, had been taking part in a Police Week which included visits by the underwater search team in May 1982.

Leicester's traffic wardens getting ready for 1 June 1965, the day they would be able to direct and control traffic. Christopher Wren gives instruction at the City Police HQ. The wardens are, left to right: Faith Walton, William Clarke, Percy Boulter and David Cufflin.

Wardens on wheels: Leicester Traffic Wardens are now equipped with mopeds. Left to right: Robert Searle, Jane Wright, Harold Pearce, Hedley Key, seen here in June 1966.

Traffic wardens Jane Allison (left) and Alison Stapleford claim another 'victim' on 27 March 1986.

Leicester prison officer Mr Rockford Pratt came across an interesting find while clearing up at work. He discovered an old picture of the prison officers' houses which probably dates back to about 1890. It was taken by F. W. Broadhead, photographers of 55 Welford Road, Leicester, but Mr Pratt has been unable to trace the firm. Several changes have taken place since the photograph was taken. The grounds have been made into a car park, the ivy from the prison officers' houses has been removed, and of course, the prison uniform – worn by the man in the picture – has changed.

Leicester Prison exercise yard in June 1955. Under the eye of a uniformed officer, prisoners sew mailbags in the open air. Almost everything produced by prison labour went to the Services or Government departments. Faces were blacked out to avoid identification.

A 'Black Maria' prison van pulls up at the gates to Leicester Prison to unload prisoners in August 1955.

A passing *Leicester Mercury* cameraman took this through-the-windscreen picture of the latest motorcade arriving at Leicester Prison, this time with two men from Durham for the maximum security unit. They had police and prison officer escorts in Panda cars, and a security blanket was provided, from the county boundary, by Leicester and Rutland Police officers, in May 1968.

Transports of Delight

Busy times: This picture shows the blacksmith's shop in the heart of the city, near the Mitre and Keys public house. It is believed that the picture was taken towards the end of the last century.

The Wigston blacksmith's forge with an array of horseshoes hanging from nails above the door.

Delivering the milk in 1916.

Pictured in the early days of World War One, Miss Miriam Bakewell, the first woman to be employed by H. Johnson & Co to drive a baker's cart. She emigrated to Australia following her marriage in 1919.

Selling fruit around the villages was a job for the horse and cart. This picture was taken outside Groby School. The barrow, called a 'Nottingham Barrow', belonged to Billy Raynes and was made during the latter part of the 19th century. The horse – Old Bill – was said to be an ex-Army horse and is pictured with Mr George Rayns. At the time of the photograph, bananas were five for threepence (1½p today), oranges 50 for one shilling (5p in today's currency), eating apples 4lbs for sixpence (2½p), cooking apples the equivalent of 1p per lb.

A turn-of-the century horse-drawn bread wagon, which delivered Headley's award-winning loaves around Leicester.

This is believed to be the last privately-owned brougham used in Leicester. It belonged to the late Mr J. B. Everard when he lived in Knighton Park Road. The picture was taken in 1921 and on the box seat is Mr Ernest Guilford, 507 Welford Road, who was the Lord Mayor's chauffeur from 1926 to 1947. He drove the last Mayor, Alderman Thomas Walker, and 20 Lord Mayors. Mr John Breedon Everard belonged to the firm of Pick, Everard, Keay & Gimson, architects and civil engineers. He was associated with the building of Leicester Cattle Market, the making of Swithland Reservoir and many other works for the Water Committee.

Father Christmas arrives in Leicester in a stage coach. This picture shows him passing along Humberstone Gate in November 1937.

With fuel for vehicles virtually unobtainable except for vital war work, the lady uses horse power to get around. She is tethering her pony and trap to a lamp post in Town Hall Square in August 1942.

The Lord Mayor and Lady Mayoress, Alderman and Mrs C. R. Keene, took part in a procession of historic transport. In this hansom cab they rode in the procession before going to the reopening of the Newarke Houses Museum in May 1953.

The Coombes on their way to Melton's shopping centre in February 1956 in their pony and trap.

A gipsy procession on Aylestone Road, going to Loughborough Fair in November 1950. The donkeys seem to have a road sense of their own.

Breakfast time by the side of the road near Anstey – a favourite resting place for gipsies. Children are gathered round the fire while father prepares the meal, in April 1952.

"Just keep close to mother," was the whinnied advice given, no doubt, to this colt before the two horses and their caravan ventured along busy streets of Leicester. And the youngster appears to have taken notice. For never once did he skip about amid the traffic to cause 'mum' worry, as their owner directed them through the city for the open road in May 1954.

A rag and bone man's horse waits patiently outside this hostelry in Thurcaston Road in September 1969.

With rings on her fingers, her brown hair braided and pinned-up, Anna Snutch in the stable style doorway of her gipsy wagon in May 1956.

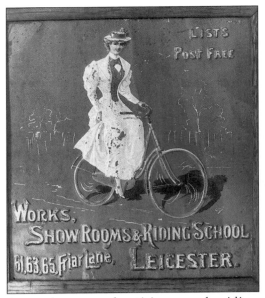

A metal poster advertising a cycle riding school in Friar Lane about the turn of the century.

Two keen cyclists, Miss Winifred Percy (in foreground) and a friend. Miss Percy was a well-known teacher in Leicester. The picture is about 1900.

The Victor Early Morning Ramblers pose with their bicycles in Abbey Park at the turn of the century.

'Stop Me and Buy One.' This ice-cream seller's tricycle in 1930 displays ice-cream for sale at twopence, sixpence, and one shilling for ice bricks and fourpence for a tub. The rider is Mr Walter Percy Markillie, who would have been glad to do any job during the Depression.

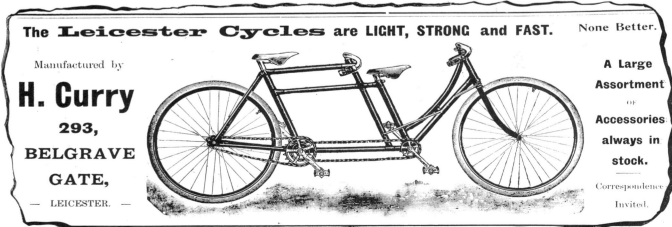

A Curry's advertisement in the *Leicestershire Cricket and Athletic Annual* for 1897.

A pre-1920 Premier Motorcycle belt-driven with a single-cylinder engine. The headlamp is lit by acetylene gas from a carbide generator.

The Syston Foxes, one of the teams of 'skid kids' in Sunday's church parade in Leicester in May 1954.

Good fun isn't it? But these happy young people, larking about in 1926, wouldn't have gone far without running into trouble nowadays, when three people on one motorcycle amounts to a serious road traffic offence and the same applies to towing a cyclist. At the time, that didn't worry Mr Richard Walne, of North Avenue, Leicester, (left), his sister Winifred, and two brothers Russell and Sydney (now dead) who were off to Woodhouse Eaves.

Mr Leslie Wilford of Wigston Lane, Aylestone pictured in the centre of this photograph riding a 350cc Velocette in a track event near Lutterworth in 1929.

Father Leonard Sheil on a BSA C11 of the late 1940s, pictured in 1954.

In April 1958, the unsettled Easter Sunday weather did not deter these members of the Leicester Motor Scooter Club setting off from their Humberstone Gate meeting place for a tour of Rutland.

A 1906 Clyde, the only car to be manufactured in Leicester.

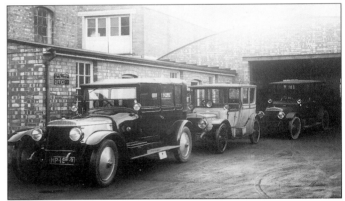

St Mary's Motor Co Ltd garage of Market Harborough, seen here in the 1920s with a brand new limousine and two others in for repair.

Highfields Garage on St Peter's Road in January 1950 with Mr Watts putting up posters for unrationed motor fuel.

In July 1953 this petrol filling station could easily spoil the pastoral beauty of Newtown Linford, so the parish council demanded that, so that the pumps would be in keeping with the street, a little thatch should be added. And with flower baskets, too, it looks well. The thatch was Norfolk reed.

Memories… Jim Lapworth

The original Lapworth shop in 1920, with Edith in the doorway and Arthur at the horse and cart.

A COUPLE of rolls of lino, the old woodspring mattresses, an old-fashioned clothes mangle, coal and chamber pots.

That used to be part of the typical household load, when Leicester removal firm E. E. Lapworth & Sons started business in 1920.

No carpets then for the typical city home, and of course no washing machines, no fridges, no televisions.

"That was when we started up in Leamington Street, off Narborough Road North," says Jim Lapworth, one of two Lapworths still working in the family firm today (the other is Jim's cousin, John Lapworth).

"We had an off-licence which my grandmother Edith ran, and a haulage business which my grandfather Arthur ran. All the horses and carts were kept behind that gateway you can just see to the right of the old photograph."

In those early days,

The five Lapworth brothers who were partners in the family firm. They are (left to right) Ambrose, Leonard, George, Maurice and Jack.

house removals were carried out with a horse and dray, or pony and trolley.

It cost 3s 6d an hour, or 6s if you wanted two men. The 'tip' might be a box of matches.

But Lapworth's really moved up a gear when Arthur bought a new lorry – a Model T Ford – in 1923. It cost him £120.

The advantage was speed as well as capacity. The company had a contract to carry hosiery from a factory in Leicester to a factory in Countesthorpe.

With their new vehicle, they could manage three loads a day, instead of one.

"The lorry used to do market runs too," says Jim. "It might take strawberries from the train to the market. We also had a contract to deliver coke to Leicester Prison."

Over the years, more lorries were added, and also more Lapworths. All five of Arthur's sons eventually joined the business.

Vehicles have got bigger and bigger, says Jim, a third generation removal man. And travelling has got easier and easier.

"In the old days, if you went up to the north of Scotland, you'd be out for well over a week. Even quite recently, it would take nine hours to get up to Scotch Corner on the old A1.

"Now you can get to Glasgow and back in one night, if you have to. The only restriction is the hours you're allowed to drive."

As for the worldly goods, they have changed too down the years.

Jim Lapworth and a removal team today at Lapworth's of Leicester.

Jim says, "At one time nearly every job involved a ladder up to the window, because heavy furniture wouldn't come down the stairs.

"There are actually less really bulky items now, but people have got different things like deep freezers and music centres and computers.

And the most difficult thing to move? "Pianos can be tricky. But the worst thing we had recently was a huge wooden bed.

"The customer had altered the stairs since it was put in, and it just wouldn't go down. So – under his instructions – we had to saw the whole thing in half, and transport it in two big pieces!"

Mr J. Walker of Great Bowden preparing for the Fernie Car Club Rally in Market Harborough in November 1953.

The Lord Mayor of Leicester's Rolls-Royce Phantom 6 – £13,800 of gleaming-black paintwork – was in a collision with a humble Ford – and lost. It happened at 4.40pm on Swain Street Bridge, only ten minutes after chauffeur Mr Thomas Dickman had dropped off the Lord Mayor, Alderman Percy Watts. He had been to a meeting at the Trinity Hospital. The front offside wing of the Rolls was stove in, and unofficial estimates put the cost of repair at around £1,000. The Anglia estate car was slightly damaged. With Rolls-Royce ABC 1 out of action, the second official car took over, Austin Princess 1 ABC. The Rolls was purchased in January 1970 and created some controversy because of its cost.

"Er … you can't park there!" This Morris 1000 van managed to leap over a three-foot high wall and crash into the Magazine in Newarke Street, coming to rest against one of the cannons. It was later removed by crane in January 1972. The number plate 'BYE' seems to sum it all up!

Something a little more sedate. Northgate Locks, Frog Island, 1908. Notice the women's head-dress and costume.

An Auster Autocraft built at Rearsby in 1945 which was bought by Leicester Museums for £700 in 1969. Seen here are the pilot (right) Mr Philip Goodwin. His two passengers are Mr Bonlan (left), Director of Museums, and Mr J. Wood, Keeper of Technology at the Museum. The single-engined Auster Autocar were produced between 1950 and 1957 – 82 were built at Rearsby. Altogether 3,607 Austers were built between 1939 and 1965.

Crowds line the towpath to look at the boats during the Inland Waterways Rally held at Market Harborough in August 1950.

Tickets Please

Tram track laying for electric car operations on 22 September 1903. They came into service in May the following year.

These children seem to be more interested in the photographer and unaware of the traffic in this 1905 photograph opposite London Road Railway Station.

Leicester trams with 'Welcome Home' on the side in September 1910, recalling 'The Leicester Homecoming, the first event of its kind promoted in the UK', which brought back many of the town's sons and daughters – particularly those who had emigrated to the US – on a return visit.

Electric trams in busy Gallowtree Gate in 1938.

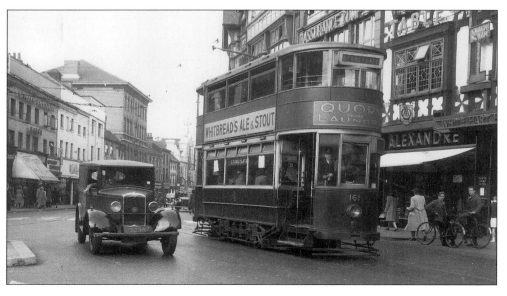

A tramcar passes the White Hart Hotel on 21 September 1949. Trams were to finish running on the streets of Leicester six weeks later, on 9 November.

In March 1950, City transport workers removing copper wire in Granby Street after the end of the tram era. Leicester had 20 miles of track and 40 miles of overhead wire. The tower wagon dates from 1911 and has been preserved.

A Midland Red conductor awaiting passengers on the Countesthorpe service outside the Magazine in 1935. The College of Art and Technology stands behind.

A 1930s view of Oadby at Burton's corner where The Parade at Oadby joins the A6 to Great Glen. Oadby Furnishers now stands on this corner.

Applegate Street in November 1945, showing tram and bus.

An elderly lady about to board a Midland Red bus on a misty morning on Aylestone Road on 27 November 1945.

Welford Place with queues for buses home after work on Welford Road at the junction with Belvoir Street, Pocklingtons Walk and Newarke Street. The photograph was taken from the roof of the Leicester Permanent Building Society on 12 October 1946.

Traffic negotiates the Granby Halls Island in January 1950. Leicester Prison dominates the background.

A check point on London Road during a three-day census in August 1955. Some 150 young men and women on vacation are helping the Corporation and Ministry of Transport plan tomorrow's roads.

London Road at the junction with Evington Road in August 1957. The building to the left was Mann Egerton's and is now a bank.

An Austin A35 grabs the last parking space on the corner of Station Street where it joins London Road on a cold November day in 1960 as the delivery boy struggles to get out of town on his bicycle.

Christmas shoppers and workers making their way home outside Lewis's Store in December 1971.

In November 1959 traffic speeds along the newly-opened M1. This picture was taken from the A45 flyover, looking northwards. Notice there is no central reservation (barriers) and the small amount of vehicles.

Leicester's London Road Railway Station pictured at the turn of the century.

The Great Central Railway Station pictured around 1925.

Over 85 years ago, Leicester had a railway strike that saw the Army called in. The strike began on 17 August 1911 and that night, a special train arrived bringing soldiers of the Royal West Surrey Regiment to Leicester. They were quartered at Glen Parva and confined to barracks until 19 August when an ugly incident occurred at London Road Station. A milk cart was overturned and the station-master asked for help. The soldiers took over guarding the signal boxes, the goods yards and the station. After a further two days, the strike was over and Leicester's railways returned to normal.

Passengers are informed of the latest news during the January 1924 rail strike.

A railway accident at Leicester on 29 February 1912. The engine has remained upright with the help of supports, while the tender rests on the pavement below.

The driver and fireman of the Royal Train, both Leicester men – H. S. Barraclough and E. N. Newman – in the cab of Royal Scot Class locomotive 6128 *The Lovat Scouts* which had been rebuilt not long before this photograph was taken on 30 October 1946.

Picturesque Lowesby Station pictured in August 1951 as station staff ten their floral displays.

Overlooking the engine shed and sidings and known to trainspotters as 'The Birdcage', this footpath bridge is an offshoot of Swain Street Bridge. The footpath is laid over a cantilever structure, starting at about 30 feet from the level of the railway and forms part of Hutchinson Street. It is pictured here in February 1954.

Three railwaymen coming on duty at London Road Station on a wet day in January 1955. The locomotive behind is an Ivatt 2-6-2 tank.

A Black Five locomotive with its front embedded in the Meadow Lane Bridge at Loughborough in March 1958.

Pictured in August 1958, Leicester Motive Power Depot with a variety of engines in the yard, including, in the foreground, ex-Midland Railway '2p' 4-4-0 No 40452.

Resist change urges the poster, but it did not help the fate of this bridge which carried the Great Central at Northgates and which was later demolished.

A diesel pulls into London Road Station in October 1962. The canopy has now gone, leaving an open station.

The train now standing at Platform 3 – at Leicester's London Road Station – is the APTE (Advanced Passenger Train Experiment) which was on a trial run from Derby in August 1973.

Memories… Ray Martin

RAY Martin had always been mad on steam trains. So it was no real surprise to anyone when he started work on the railways in 1950 – Beale Street MPD (Motive Power Depot) in Leicester, to be precise.

"It was a 32-road roundhouse," he explained. "That's two roads in, and a big turntable with 32 roads off for stabling the engines."

He worked for nine months as a cleaner, a broad job which also involved shovelling coal, shovelling ash, and travelling down to Wigston every Sunday to stack all the coal reserves into heaps about eight feet high.

"Wigston South was a major rail junction then," he recalls. "There was an enormous signal box there, and a vast gantry of signals."

He also vividly remembers a 'busman's holiday' to Crewe, where as a 16-year-old he posed with a friend on the splendid *Duchess of Hamilton* – a Coronation Class 462 Pacific, number 46229.

But he wasn't a cleaner for long. He took and passed the tests to be a fireman.

"You have to know about firing techniques, parts of the boiler and fire box and about safety. You're the driver's eyes and ears, because there's very poor visibility on a steam locomotive."

In 1951, he was a fireman on the Fox Street Jocko, a shunting engine that picked up coaching stock at the London Road Station in Leicester, and stabled them in the nearby sidings.

By 1955, after National Service, he got 'my rightful place' in The Links. "I finished on the top passenger link, on expresses to London St Pancras.

"But we went everywhere, all over the place, different engines every day from a big roster board mounted on the wall and made up every day by the Running Foreman."

Usually a steam raiser started the fire up. When Ray arrived, his job was to get the steam up to working

Ray Martin (on the right) with a friend on the *Duchess of Hamilton* at Crewe, in 1950. (Note the train number.)

Now he's the boss. Ray more than 40 years later gets to drive the *Duchess of Hamilton* at last, on the Great Central Railway.

pressure, and check coal and water levels.

But by the late 1950s, the diesels were arriving, and Ray wasn't interested in diesels. He left to join Post Office Telecommunictions.

Although a fireman occasionally takes over driving a train, Ray was never an official engine driver.

But that wasn't the end of his career with steam trains. When the Great Central Railway, which now runs from Loughborough to north of Leicester, re-opened as a tourist attraction, Ray was there as a volunteer helper.

He started as a cleaner again in 1990, but this time he had his sights set even higher. This time he

was going to be a driver.

He passed his exams. In fact his examiner told him "if you can't drive the ****** Ray, then no one can".

"Oh yes, I love it," he says. "There's nothing like steam. The excitement, the noises, the smell of steam and hot oil, there's an atmosphere. It's the closest a machine gets to a living being."

And more than 40 years after starting in the railways, Ray got to drive engines at last.

And one of them was the *Duchess of Hamilton*, a Coronation Class 462 Pacific, number 46229. The same one he had posed longingly on as a teenager more than 40 years before. And here are the pictures to prove it!

Aircraft on the spot. Ratby Engineering Works' offices are on Desford Aerodrome, so directors Mr T. E. Boynton and Mr W. G. Turnbull have only to walk across to the hangers to reach their aircraft in November 1951.

Fog gradually closes in around Viscount G-ASNC, shortly after its return to East Midlands Airport, Castle Donington, in November 1971.

A Roof Over Our Heads

A Leicester street in the 1920s – living conditions could be grim.

A 1930s view of Saffron Lane with new houses on one side of the road, the other side would follow later.

This photograph, taken at 12.30pm on Thursday, 13 February 1936, shows a yard off South Bond Street. People lived in these appalling conditions only 60 years ago. Notice the communal tap in the middle of the yard.

Slums in 1951. Eleven people lived in this house.

Lead Street in April 1952 was not an isolated instance of slum conditions in Leicester. Especially in St Margaret's Ward there were too many streets, unseen by the majority, where families lacked amenities which today are considered essential.

The tiny backyards of houses in Wharf Street in July 1954.

Pictured in April 1956, Mrs Pethers and her three children, Terence (10), Michael (4) and Averil (2) in the cheerless, sunless yard which provides the only access to her house and the only place where the children can play. Behind is the window of the living room, which admits so little natural light that they have to keep the electric light on all day.

What an immensely satisfying sight for four Leicester youngsters. Under the Wharf Street redevelopment scheme, Christow Street Infants' School was coming down. The school, built during the 1870s by Leicester School Board, used to accommodate about 130 pupils but had only 30 when it closed in December 1955. The four taking a last look at their old school are (left to right): Philip Wright (six), 66 Gladstone Street; Michael Wright (seven) 56 Crafton Street; Gerald Frape (nine), 21 Brougham Street; and Terry Wright (eight), 72 Gladstone Street. All four were then pupils of Taylor Street School.

In direct contrast to some earlier pictures, Mr Albert Stretton reads a newspaper in the comfortable front room of his daughter's bungalow at Clarke's Allotments off Melton Road in January 1956.

A view from St John's Church in June 1956. To the right is South Albion Street, being demolished. In the foreground is Slawson Street.

A chimney crashes to the ground during slum clearance operations in the Peel Street area of Leicester in January 1958.

Abbey Gate, part of the 1960s slum clearance programme.

England were just about to win the World Cup when this picture was taken in April 1966. It shows that even as recently as 30 odd years ago, people were living in squalid conditions in Leicester. In this six-roomed terraced house at 24 Jackson Street, the tap had only cold water.

Memories... Doll Sharratt

SHE worked as a post-machinist in Brevit's Shoe factory near the city centre.

So Doris 'Doll' Sharratt, now 84, actually watched the 1960s 24-storey St Matthew's flats rise up day by day from ground level.

Doll Sharratt (right) and sister-in-law Phyllis White.

"I said 'I'd like to live in one of them'" she remembers. "We were living in Braunstone at the time, but the house and garden were getting too much for my husband and me. "These new flats, they seemed very modern. The way of the future. So I just kept going on at the council to let us move into one. I had to torment them!"

Doll eventually got her way. She moved into the 19th floor not too long after the flats were opened in 1968.

"It was flats for elderly people at first, and it seemed ever so quiet – a nice quiet place to live. And I've never regretted it since. From my flat on a good day I can see right across to Bradgate Park.

"The only time I don't like it is when it's thundering and lightning!"

It seems a long way from one of Leicester's tallest buildings to the city house where Doll was born.

"I lived in Grecian Street in St Marks, until I got married when I was 23. We had a three-bedroom terraced house, but they were very tiny rooms. Me and my sister shared one bed in the smallest bedroom.

"We had a tap in the house, but no bathroom of course. The toilet was outside, up the yard, shared between two families.

"The house was heated by coal, in an old-fashioned fireplace. We had a gas stove, though. Lighting got better, first gas lighting, then electric."

Then Doll got married, and the couple moved to a one up, one down in Pasture Lane, Leicester. "Yes, that was a tiny house. Everything was in the living room!"

And then the couple moved out to Braunstone, and a three-bedroom house with a garden in Wilmore Crescent.

"They were very nice, they were. And Braunstone was lovely when we first went up there. People were really neighbours then. They'd do anything for anybody."

From one point of view, Doll is convinced that her present high-rise flat is the best accommodation she has ever had.

"Housing has just improved and improved as I've got older. In the old days we had no bathroom, no proper heating. And the jobs like cooking and cleaning are much easier now.

"And now we have our televisions, where in the old days you had a

Still dominating: The flats today.

wireless and that was it. And you were lucky if you had got one of them."

Another thing Doll likes is the security of these flats. "It's really good. You're not frightened to go around. You feel safe."

But perhaps there is one thing missing.

"I go in and shut my door, and that's it. You don't see a soul. You can't have a street going upwards, so unless you make an effort to mix, you can get lonely."

As Doll's case shows, housing has improved physically beyond recognition through this century. But socially? That's debatable.

The high-rise flats in St Matthews, Leicester, when they were first built in 1968.

A panoramic view of the city skyline showing the Gas Works and floodlights of Leicester City Football Club at Filbert Street. In th

oreground are the houses and shops of Mill Lane. The photograph was taken from The Gateway in January 1961.

Childhood Memories

Young donkey riders at the turn of century in Abbey Park.

Mrs P. M. Goodacre (right), pictured here with her three sisters, applauded the efforts of a Mr and Mrs Robson to bring gymnastics to working class youngsters in the days before World War One. Every Tuesday-Thursday nights, classes were held at swimming baths in Spence Street, Cossington Street and Bath Lane. It was thought to be too cold to swim during the winter months so all the baths were boarded over and about 80 or so attended the classes, a few pence being charged for a two-hour session.

Belgrave High School in 1923, in the days long before the Comprehensive system.

Ice-cream on Christmas morning nearly 70 years ago, in the cobbled street at the junction of Albion Street and Chatham Street.

Three youngsters wondering if they dare take a drink from the landlord's pump at the Coach and Horses, Kibworth, in May 1938.

Avenue Road Infants' School, in 1951 with a class of 43 pupils, common in those days, because of the 'baby boom' at the end of World War Two.

Memories... John Moyler

THE young boy's nose poked out from the prison camp blankets into the bitter North China air. His eyes caught the glistening little decorations on the small bare branch, wrapped with green paper.

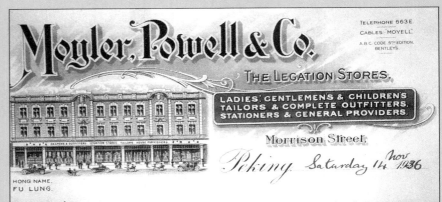

The letterhead of Moyler, Powell & Co, the shop run by Arthur Moyler in Morrison Street, Peking.

John Moyler at his Leicester home, with his prison camp puppets.

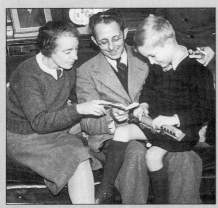

Young John with his parents Arthur and Eileen.

And then, after two big hugs from his parents, he saw the home-made Punch and Policeman glove puppets, and the draughts board.

This was Christmas Day more than 50 years ago and more than 5,000 miles away for John Moyler.

It was Christmas in Weihsien – for young John spent much of his childhood as one of 2,000 prisoners of all ages in a Japanese prison camp during World War Two.

"We kids had learnt by now not to expect very much at Christmas," recalls Mr Moyler, a former department store carpenter who now lives in Aylestone, Leicester.

"But I had glove puppets lovingly made by my parents from scraps of clothes. And the draughts were hand made too – a broom handle somewhere must have been shorter!"

Mr Moyler remembers that his Christmas Day breakfast was Goalag – a rough maize porridge bread, and – luxury – a black market egg.

And then he was a very small, very still Cock Robin in a theatrical production of Who Killed Cock Robin?

The Moyler family had owned a department store in Peking before the war, and were well-off, with a cook, domestic staff and a nanny.

Then came Pearl Harbor, and the Japanese marched into China, and for foreign nationals everything changed overnight.

At first the Moyler family was kept under guard in the British Embassy in Peking.

But by 1943 young John – with parents Arthur and Eileen – were imprisoned in a ramshackle Presbyterian mission compound 200 miles south-east of Peking.

"I remember arriving at the camp and wondering who those thin, scruffy people were inside it," he recalls. "Of course, after a few days, we looked just the same."

He remembers the camp's terrible food: "If the stew was over-seasoned, you knew something in it must have gone off."

And he remembers the children daring each other to go into the mortuary, to see if anyone had died that day.

"One of the people who died in Weihsien was Eric Liddell, the man who wouldn't run on Sunday in Chariots of Fire. He went on to be a missionary in China."

But most of all he remembers the pieces of paper fluttering down from American planes, to tell the scarecrow prisoners that the war was over.

"We were ecstatic, absolutely crazy, shouting, swearing and hugging each other."

Survivors were eventually taken to Hong Kong – "by then dad weighed 6st 10lb, and mum weighed 5st".

"Many Christmases have come and gone since then," said Mr Moyler. "But there was something special about that Christmas in Weihsien."

And from on old cardboard box on a winter's night in his Leicester semi, he produces the glove puppets and the draughts, lovingly made by his mum and dad in a prison camp in China, which he has kept all these years.

"Camp training," he smiled. "Never throw anything away..."

To the younger generation the pump is more attractive than the tap. In this picture Wayne Cannon holds the bucket while Barbara West works the handle of the Fleckney pump in June 1952.

The New Parks House Infants' School pictured just after it opened in March 1950. It took 18 months longer and £23,000 more to build than was originally estimated. The need for it was so urgent, however, that part of it was in use as a school long before the builders left. Until the New Parks Community Centre was opened later that year, it was the only building available for public meetings on the estate, and was also used as a Sunday School and community centre as well as a day school.

At 7am on 13 July 1957, the Revd George Brian, Vicar of St Leonard's Church, Leicester, began a 12-hour 'sitting marathon' to raise funds for the Church's 80th birthday building restoration £600 appeal. Mr Brain, seen here receiving gifts from children of the parish, sat in the church porch to welcome all-comers.

Members of the 12th Leicester Scouts pictured in 1929. Standing, back row (left to right): K. Armstrong, J. McPhee, Sid Allen (Scout master), Golland (senior), the Revd R. Johnson, R. Mackrory, D. C. Williams (assistant Scout master), R. Woolman, Thompson, D. Butler, J. Lee. Middle row: B. Salt, Warren, E. Johnson, B. Newton, A. McKenzie, H. Moffat, R. Biddles. Front row: W. Ratcliffe, K. Robertson, W. Flewitt, R. Garfoot, Golland (junior).

Scouts of the 90th Leicester (St Anne's) checking over their car, *Tin Annie*, for the Midland Area Scouts' Soapbox Derby, staged at Coventry in June 1953. They are (left to right) Douglas Oakes, Brian Povoas, John Pether, Terence Baines and Garth Pratt.

Remember Y-Z Chewing gum for 1d a packet? This lad wishes he could reach one in November 1957.

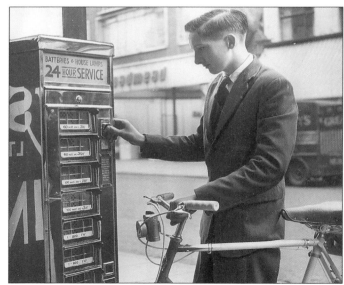

In October 1961, a vending machine which gave a 24-hour service to householders and cyclists had recently been installed outside a Leicester cycle shop. The eight-compartment machine carried house electric light bulbs, cycle and torch batteries and bulbs.

Leicester at War

For Queen and Country …London Road is lined with people gathered to welcome the Leicestershire Yeomanry home from the war in South Africa in 1902. A grand day for the parade, judging by the summery boaters and parasols. The troops are marching past Highfield Street towards Victoria Park.

Troops marching along Granby Street to the unveiling ceremony in Town Hall Square in December 1909. Many of them would no doubt have served in South Africa.

The scene at the unveiling of the South African War Memorial statues in December 1909 in Town Hall Square. First in the group on the right-hand side is the High Sheriff (Colonel Dalgliesh), looking remarkably like King Edward VII. With him are the Mayor of Loughborough (Alderman Coltman), Major Freer, the Mayor of Leicester (Alderman Lakin). Next to Alderman Lakin is Mr Sam Groocock, Leicester's mace-bearer for many years and who lived in Dorchester Road, and behind Mr Groocock, in peaked cap, is Police Superintendent Geary. By the memorial are Canon Sanders, who was vicar of St Martin's and the Revd Atkins.

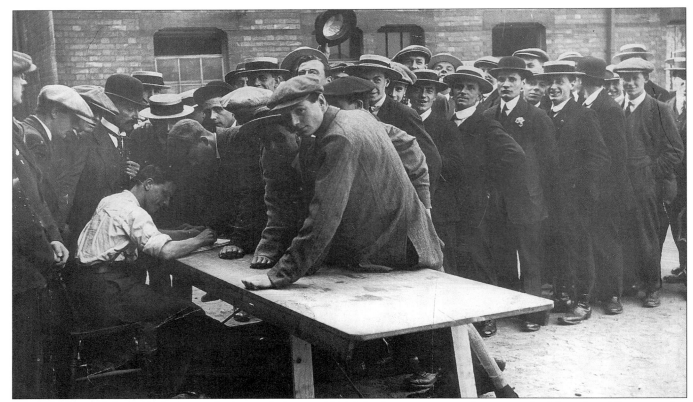

The call to arms is heard in Leicester during early August 1914. Mostly young men volunteer at the Magazine. All wear smiles …it'll all be over by Christmas.

Rifles are issued, uniforms will follow. The Magazine parade ground resounds to the crunch of boots. A 'contemptible little army' is on the march.

Salute: King George V inspects his troops in Leicester.

May Day in Leicester Market Place in 1916 with Ramsay MacDonald, then MP for Leicester, and later to become Prime Minister twice, persuading his vast audience that conscription, which had just come in, was not the intolerable infringement of liberty that many ILP men claimed it to be in those days.

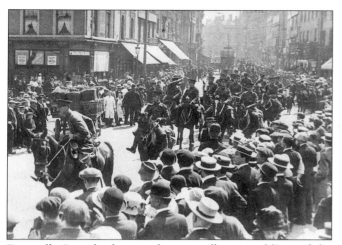

Farewell: Crowds cheer and say goodbye to soldiers of the Leicestershire Yeomanry in Granby Street, Leicester, as they go off to war.

Kiss: A soldier from the Leicestershire Regiment says goodbye to a child as he leaves for the horror of war.

The Leicester resting somewhere on the Western Front against a backdrop of war. Passed by the censor, the picture's original caption says: 'A well-deserved rest for a meal, showing "Tommy" as a picture of contentment.'

16 Company, No 2 Section of the Machine Gun Corps, Leicestershire Regiment, photographed at a farm on the Cassel-Wormhout road, France, in April 1916. Ernest E. Neale, is sixth from the right, back row. He joined the 1st Battalion, Leicestershire Regiment in December 1912, at the early age of 16½ and served in Ireland before the regiment moved to France in September 1914, thus becoming a member of the elite 'Old Contemptibles'. The regiment took part in numerous battles including the Aisne, First Ypres and the Hooge, and in September 1915 Mr Neale was awarded the Cross of St George, 4th Class, a gallantry award founded in 1769 by the Empress Catherine of Russia and abolished in 1917 after the Russian Revolution. He was awarded the Military Medal in 1916, at the age of 20, and was also Mentioned in Despatches on four occasions. After the war, he obtained his discharge from the Regular Army, having risen to the rank of Company Sergeant Major, and served a further seven years on the Army Reserve.

Sergeant Boulter VC (extreme left), seen here at Wigston on 9 December 1916 during a parade.

A convoy of army ambulances taking away wounded servicemen at Leicester London Road Station during World War One.

Campbell Street railway sidings, Leicester, sees the homecoming of those who caught 'a bit of Blighty'. Perhaps they were the lucky ones.

More wounded are coming home to Leicester during 'the war to end wars'.

War wounded outside the Pavilion Theatre, Leicester, awaiting a charity performance of *The Somerset Girl*. Judging by their cap badges they were men of all regiments from all parts of the British Isles. One soldier, presumably a member of the Anzac forces, wears the once-familiar hat with one side upright to the crown.

Wartime wedding on 17 June 1917, the day Mr Batt married Miss Ball. The picture was taken outside the bride's parents' shop in Down Street, Melton Road, Leicester. Cricket, alas, played a tragic role in the life of Mr Batt and Miss Ball. The bride's younger brother, Arthur (the boy sitting on the left), was killed during a game on Victoria Park when he was struck on the temple by a ball and died immediately. The soldier on the extreme left is Staff Sergeant Lake of the Leicestershire Regiment, who was later landlord of the Balmoral Arms in Belgrave Road. The soldier seated is Private G. Ball of the RAMC.

Women munition workers producing shells at Coalville during World War One.

Colonel R. Dalgliesh speaking from the top of a tank in Town Hall Square in January 1918.

A Leicestershire hero home from the war, with a number of admiring small boys.

Armistice celebrations in November 1918: Here we see some local ladies with Union Flags ready to take part in the proceedings.

Memories ...Don Green

MOST people go to war with a uniform, a gun and a head full of glory.

Don Green had all those of course – he was desperately keen to be a soldier. But he also had paper, pens and pencils.

One of Don Green's World War Two drawings, 'The German in the Orchard'.

Don Green aged 19 in his Queen's 7th Armoured Division uniform.

For while most veterans can only use their memories to paint a picture of what the war was like, Don can turn to his illustrated diary.

"The truth is, war can contain long periods of intense boredom," Don claims. "So I kept every scrap of paper I could find, and drew the cartoons and wrote the diary to help pass the time."

So we can actually see Don's versions of World War Two, from when he landed in France the day after D-Day, to his two 'lost weeks' after he was put out of action.

"We made the beach and started the business of invading the joint," says his diary for 10 June 1944, at the start of 19-year-old Mr Green's personal war.

"Not much fun," recalls Don today, from his home in Wigston. "Our little landing craft was knocked all over the place by the big ships either side.

"And I decided it would be safer to jump over the side rather than run down the ramp, so my first few steps in France were underwater!"

Many of his sketches blend the horrific and the mundane. For example, one dated 18 July 1944, shows two army mates – Johnny Ludford and George Richardson – strolling casually by a dead enemy soldier, arm outstretched.

"The German in the Orchard," notes the caption. "Later buried by two Jocks on small verge at foot of wall."

As the Queen's/7th Armoured Division zig-zagged across France, Don remembers loving the cheese, hating the shelling, and meeting a very mixed reaction from the French locals.

"Remember we had probably knocked out their village before advancing," he explained. "They certainly weren't all pleased to see us."

A low point was being trapped in an orchard at Villers Bocage. "There was a German behind every hedge and tree, but we couldn't see them and they couldn't see us. It was terrifying."

But Don's direct part in the war was destined to last just seven weeks.

"I was buried underneath a collapsed wall that was hit by a shell," he says. "And that was the end of the action for me.

"I don't know if it was shell shock or what it was, but the next two weeks when I was in hospital are completely blank. Two lost weeks."

Don Green works on his latest cartoon, at his home in Wigston.

All he remembers – and that perhaps because he was reminded later – is flooring a hospital orderly with a bedside table, late at night.

"I must have thought I was back in the trenches," he says.

Fortunately the artistic soldier made a full recovery, and spent the rest of the war in England.

And today he still works with pens and paper – as a cartoonist for magazines and 'anyone who'll pay me!'.

Still drawing on his experience, you could say.

And lest we forget: the gravestone of Lance-corporal S. P. Good of the Leicestershire Regiment, who was only 19 when he was killed only two weeks after war had been declared.

Preparing for war again. A council worker paints kerbstones white so that they can be seen in the blackout.

Windows were taped to safeguard against flying glass splinters during German air-raids.

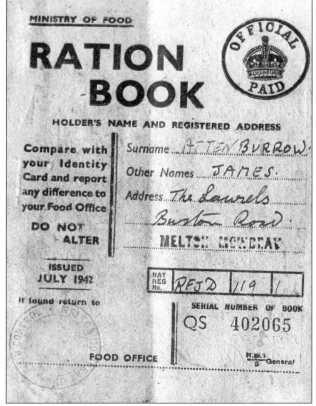

How many points have I got? Something which would become familiar to all the people of Britain from the outbreak of World War Two, right into the 1950s – the Ration Book.

Air-raid precautions exercise. Members of the public, acting as injured from a gas attack, being treated by volunteers suitably dressed for such an event.

A policeman on point duty the day after war was declared.

Bringing casualties from the LMS Loco Sheds during ARP exercises in May 1940. Germany had just invaded the Low Countries and the threat of invasion loomed.

Leicestershire sailor AB Stanley Scaman of HMS *Speedwell* with souvenir helmets which had been worn by German parachutists captured in Holland in 1940.

Leicestershire men back from Norway, which had just been invaded. "Still the old spirit – thumbs up," say these men on their way to their homes on 13 May 1940.

The Coalville contingent of the Leicestershires, who were in Norway, when they left the LNER Station to return to their unit in 1940. The sergeant kisses his wife farewell while his little son watches the cameraman.

Men of a Leicester Battery recently arrived back in England with the British Expeditionary Force which had been evacuated from Dunkirk. They were photographed 'in the Midlands' on 14 June 1940.

Soldiers of the Leicestershire Regiment and other units brought out of Dunkirk by sea were sent to Leicester and district for rest and re-equipment. This cheerful mixed group was photographed at Wigston.

Men of the 2/5th Leicester on a training march over the Scottish hills in December 1940. Only a few months previously the battalion had lost most of its men in France, but it was soon reformed and in 1943 helped to drive the Germans out of North Africa.

Cheerful waiting for the members of the Auxiliary Fire Service was soon to be replaced by sleepless days and nights. As incendiary bombs rained down on Leicester, the Fire Service was stretched to the limit.

Members of the National Fire Service in June 1941.

ARP workers searching for an old man of 80 who was buried under debris when houses in Cavendish Road, Aylestone, were bombed on 21 August 1940.

Houses on Conduit Street destroyed by enemy action on the night of 14 July 1940 when one woman was killed and seven injured. Also hit was the Midland Railway Station on London Road. There were 122 killed and 284 injured during 1940-41 Luftwaffe attacks on Leicester.

Rescue workers continue to search in the rubble in Cavendish Road for any casualties that may be buried after the raid of August 1940 in which four women, a man and a child were killed.

Soldiers examine the wreckage after one man was killed when a German bomb blasted the mud over Melton's Brook Street on 4 November 1940.

After the raid on Leicester of November 1940, the *Mercury* could report: 'After being entombed for more than 64 hours in the debris of a three-storey house which was bombed in a raid on an East Midlands town, a man whose name is understood to be Lasky, calmly gave instructions to his rescuers as to the best way to extricate him. He is seen here being removed on a stretcher.'

Although they had been bombed out of their homes in Melton, these air-raid victims still raised a smile as they carried away their personal belongings.

Freeman, Hardy & Willis shoe factory on Humberstone Road was destroyed by German bombers on 19 November 1940. Here we see firefighters dampening down early the next day.

The stark shell of Freeman Hardy and Willis' premises in Rutland Street after the bombing during the night of November 1940.

Victoria Park Pavilion, damaged by a landmine in November 1940.

When an ARP flag was hoisted at a house in Leicester near where a bomb had fallen, this little lad promptly stuck up his Union Flag alongside it.

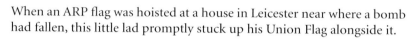

The night bombs dropped on Tollemache Avenue, Mrs Gwen Walthoe was on the Central Station: "The plane had followed the train from Nottingham to Leicester. I think they thought they had got the station but they dropped them on Tollemache Avenue. The driver managed to pull into Leicester station and he was badly shocked, because we dealt with him and I took him to the Infirmary. They fetched us out of the canteen that night and made us go under the station platform." Here workmen are clearing up as best they can.

This scene of destruction faced rescue workers and demolition squads in the Highfield Street-Tichborne Street area when night gave way to the day after the worst bombing Leicester experienced in World War Two. A total of 41 people perished when a bomb landed there in November 1940.

A young lady pretends to loot a grocery shop on London Road, while a young lad sweeps up glass after the raid on Highfields, November 1940.

The Luftwaffe helped balance the Civil Defence books by bombing the Methodist Chapel in Saxby Street. The CD used the chapel as a store for equipment until the attack on 19-20 November 1940. Mr Ted Doughty took up the story: "It had been a bad winter and a lot of volunteers had inadvertently gone home in ARP gumboots and when we came to take stock we were several hundred pairs missing. Although this was a very bad raid and it was very sad that Saxby Street Chapel should be badly damaged, it helped us out with our book-keeping because we could write off 400 pairs of gumboots 'damaged by enemy action.'"

All that remained of Kirby Muxloe Free Church after it had been struck by a bomb in the 19 November 1940 night raid.

Mr and Mrs Greenhill look over their wrecked home 'in an East Midlands town'. They were playing cards in the kitchen when a bomb dropped, but they escaped unhurt on 11 January 1941.

132

In March 1941 the *Mercury* reported: 'Ted Jordan, aged nine (left) and his brother, Frank, escaped without injury when the cottage in the East Midlands, where they had found a home after being evacuated from London, was bombed on Saturday night. After the bombing their main anxiety was that their two rabbits were buried in the debris, but next morning ARP workers found the pets unharmed in the hutch.'

Tram car No 168, representing HMS *Renown* in Leicester Warship Week, 25 February 1942. No 168 was painted to represent HMS *Renown* to encourage the citizens of Leicester to save towards the £3 million cost.

A bren gun carrier on Home Guard exercises in July 1941.

A large stock of machine tools for armament repairs at the Old Dalby Ordnance Supply Depot in April 1942.

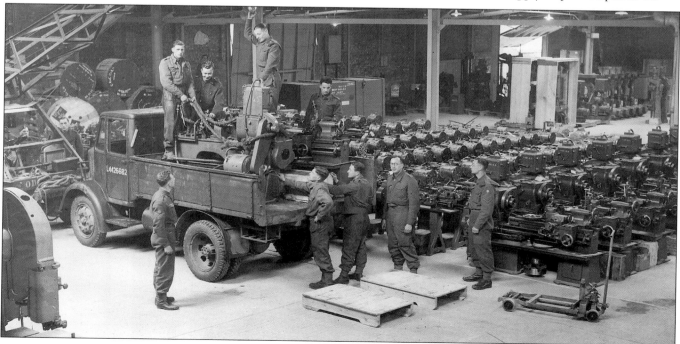

Mrs Burbidge, a National Fire Service despatch rider, pictured on her motorcycle in February 1943.

Land Girls protest – Miss Brenda Clark and Miss Alice Lippitt, representing the girls of the Women's Land Army hostel at Rearsby, who were protesting against their hostel being taken over for housing Italian PoWs, pictured arriving at the County Rooms, Leicester, to meet the County War Agricultural Executive Committee.

Because of the shortage of manpower, women were used in all varieties of war work. Miss Riley, a driver with the Royal Mail, is seen collecting letters from a post box. She was the first woman in Leicester to do this work, in January 1941.

GPO postwomen in winter uniform in March 1944.

Miss Grace Noble trimming the cabin of an Auster aircraft at Taylorcraft of Rearsby in September 1943.

A group of girls from hosiery factories in Leicester who left their work to go to an armament works, pictured in their canteen.

All girls together. A tram conductress collects fares from war workers in February 1941.

A woman loads a basket on to a wagon at a goods siding in a Leicester rail yard during the war. Women were prepared to do heavy manual work to help the war effort.

A woman rail worker checks a signal gantry in September 1942.

An ATS military policewoman examines a motorcycle despatch rider's papers at a checkpoint on 29 October 1941.

Leicester's Home Guard despatch riders on their own machines, waiting to go on a parade. Motorcycles pictured are Triumphs, BSAs and Ariels.

6 July 1942: Bringing in prisoners at Ratby during Leicester's invasion exercise in which the Home Guard and Civil Defence services co-operated.

Groby Home Guard during World War Two.

Guns from a bygone era are given up to the 'Save Metal' campaign, here being loaded on to a lorry in May 1942.

Memories... John Stafford

Bomb damage in Highfield Street, Leicester, after a World War Two air-raid.

Now living back in Belgrave, close to the street where he was born.

JOHN Stafford was born in Evans Street, Belgrave, Leicester, in 1929, the second of seven Stafford children. He lived in a terraced two-up, two-down house, and the children all slept in two beds in one bedroom.

"The two girls were head-to-toe in a single bed," recalls John, now retired after a life as a garage owner and motor mechanic.

"And us five boys were head-to-toe in a large double bed with a horsehair mattress."

John's Dad was a stoker at Leicester Gasworks, and his mother, Maggie, looked after the children, despite being increasingly ill with TB.

Food was bread and lard for breakfast, a hash for dinner and bread pudding for tea, made with stale bread from the bakers.

The Stafford's life was poor

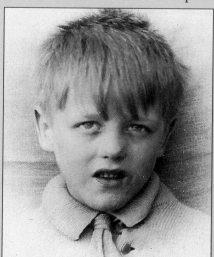

John Stafford as a boy in 1935.

enough anyway, but disaster hit the family when John's mother became too ill to look after the children, and later died.

The two girls were fostered, and the five boys went to an orphanage in Highfields, Leicester.

During World War Two, they were all choirboys at the nearby St Saviour's Church, and it is from this time that John remembers a bit of good luck at last for the Staffords. In fact, the five brothers had an amazing escape.

It was November 1940, and Leicester was experiencing its worst-ever air-raid.

The orphanage children, including the five Stafford brothers, had been ushered down to the air-raid shelter by Miss Waller, who they all called 'Mother'.

The children lay in bunks in the shelter, as loud explosions echoed across the city, and Miss Waller knitted.

A watching ARP warden told 'Mother' what happened next.

John says, "This warden had watched helplessly as a land mine on a parachute floated towards the orphanage – towards us five Staffords and the other boys and mother in the air-raid shelter. Then an astonishing thing happened.

"The parachute got caught up with the weathercock on the top of St Saviour's Church, and in doing so broke the weathercock off and it fell to the ground.

"But that diverted the land mine, which floated over us to the bottom of Grove Road.

"It landed in the middle of the road and blew up 14 houses. There were a lot of casualties." (In fact, 55 people died in this air-raid.)

"A family of four were found still sitting at a table where they had been playing cards. The blast had taken the life out of them. Other people had been buried alive in cellars.

"But although our shelter had been lifted off the ground by the blast, and was now deeply cracked all the way round the bottom, we were safe inside."

"We St Saviour's choirboys had been saved by our church's weather-cock."

Next morning, the brothers went to school as normal, with their gas masks round their necks.

"Grove Road was cordoned off," says John. "It was terrible. There were fire engines and ambulances all around, smoke and fire everywhere. The hole in the road was so big and deep it was frightening. You could have got three double decker buses into it.

"And there was the St Saviour's weathercock, about nine feet high, lying in the road."

'Bring out your aluminium pots, pans and kettles,' says the banner on this cart. And people do indeed bring out their unwanted items for the war effort.

A French mother and her children, driven from France, found a home in Leicestershire. None of them spoke English. They are pictured outside the De Montfort Hall in 1940.

A Civil Defence worker gives a helping hand to a tired little traveller upon his arrival in Leicester with a party of evacuated families from eastern coastal districts.

This little London evacuee obviously prefers to stay with the ambulance man although the bus driver is doing his best to entice her – a picture taken at Wigston when a party of people evacuated from London arrived.

The warm-hearted Americans were always looking for a practical way to show their appreciation of the welcome Leicester people, in the main, gave them. The boy holding the baseball bat sometime in 1944 is seven-year-old Billy Smith, of Guthlaxton Street, who had tragically lost a leg. The US Forces Station in Saxby Street bought him an artificial leg and when he was able to stand and walk unaided on it, provided a special uniform made by the base tailor, and gave him his own guard of honour. Among the lads pictured were four Comery brothers – Eddie, Mo, Bryan and Gerry – Peter March, and a wartime evacuee, Alfie Thompson.

"Howdy, stranger – as a matter of fact, I'm a stranger here too!" An American GI welcomes an evacuee to Leicester.

This picture shows Billy Smith taking the salute at a special inspection of US troops laid on for him. Billy had barely been able to struggle round on crutches before the GIs stepped in.

Percy Fowlks of the United States Army wrote and produced a play for the children of Barsby village. He was present at the Leicester Royal Infirmary when two of the performers, Sylvia Monaghan and Dorothy Palmer, handed over a cheque as a result of the effort.

A jeep-load of GIs of the 82nd US Airborne Division stationed at Braunstone Park, preparing to give the people of Leicester another lesson in the American way of life in 1944.

General Eisenhower inspecting troops at Stoughton Airfield, Leicester, just before D-Day in June 1944.

Children giving V-for-Victory signs on VE Day, 8 May 1945.

A street party with jubilant children celebrate VE Day.

Roll Out The Barrel

The famous Blue Boar Inn on Southgate Street in September 1959.

In what was one of old Leicester's most derelict areas was a pub called the Chelsea Pensioner. It was situated in Southgate Street, not far from Friar Lane and opposite the more famous pub of the area, the Blue Boar. This picture was taken some time around 1900, when there were still occasional palisaded homes and trees about.

The Nag's Head, Millstone Lane, Leicester (part of the Ring Road clearance scheme), pictured in September 1960.

The Old Castle Inn at Rupert's Gateway in December 1964.

The Jetty Wine Lodge as seen from the passageway between Hotel Street and Market Place. Started by the Page family in 1847, it became Yates' Wine Lodge in 1965.

Page's Wine Lodge, Leicester Market entrance in August 1965.

Wellington, author of Napoleon's defeat in Spain and at Waterloo, is second only to Nelson in the inn sign stakes. This extremely attractive design adorns the Marquis Wellington on London Road, Leicester.

The Vine Tavern which once stood at the corner of Vine Street and Elbow Lane (right of picture). Down that side of the pub is a large poster for the Theatre Royal's presentation of *A Life's Story*.

The Red Cow, an old coaching inn at Leicester Forest East on the Hinckley Road, pictured in October 1966.

On the bank of the canal lock, near where the road crosses by means of an old bridge, stands the Duke of York at Mountsorrel, seen here in the late 1940s.

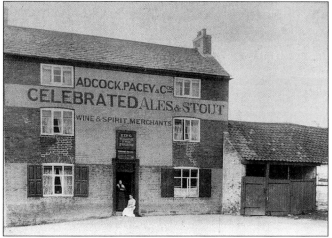

The King William IV at Barsby at the turn of the century. In the mid-1980s it was turned into a Norman fantasy, complete with suits of armour, chastity belt, and a painted copy of the Bayeux Tapestry, made by teenagers on a Youth Training Scheme.

Turret surmounted by a weathervane and an unusual roof arrangement help to provide distinctive premises for the Anchor Inn, Mountsorrel.

The Cricketer's Rest Inn at Abbey Gate in November 1955.

The Gipsy Lane Hotel in November 1951.

Only a youngster with his tin pop-gun is to be seen in this November 1950 view of Enderby High Street and the New Inn. We wonder if the little lad recognises himself today?

The Lancaster public house at Desford in the 1950s.

The White Hart in Hinckley in February 1952.

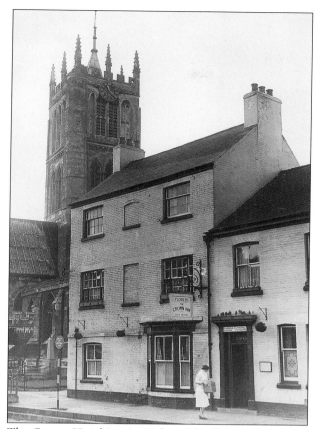

The Crown Hotel Inn in Melton Mowbray, seen here in December 1955.

Traffic moving along the Leicester to Market Harborough highway passes the sign of the Crown Inn at Great Glen in September 1951.

The Old Crown Inn, Market Harborough, which finally closed its doors in August 1957.

An old and pretty-looking inn, the Nag's Head, Harby, dates from the 17th century. It may have been a place of call for travellers using an ancient lane that cut off from The Drift and led to Nottingham. Pictured in October 1957.

An October 1951 view of the Rose and Crown in Kibworth.

The Hind Hotel in Market Harborough, which closed in 1957.

The Coach and Horses, Field Head, Markfield, in October 1951, noted as a regular venue for fox hunting meets.

In 1951 the *Mercury* said: 'Within a stone's throw of Lutterworth Parish Church is this charming pair of half-timbered houses, considered the best examples in the town. On the right is the Coach and Horses Inn, with its tiled roof, and the beauty of the more picturesque house next door is enhanced by the panelled bay windows.'

Decoratively curved gables and latticed windows provide an unusual architectural scheme for the Naseby Hotel, Gipsy Lane, Leicester.

The Joiner's Arms at Bruntingthorpe has changed little since this picture was taken in 1956.

The top end of High Street, Great Glen, in March 1961. A plaque on the houses on the right states: 'Console Cottages 1874.' They were built by Thomas Crick. Next to them is the Royal Oak which was once a bakehouse.

Over the arched doorway are the figures '1863' to mark the Nevill Arms, Medbourne, with its stone frames and latticed windows, seen here in the 1950s.

Cranoe village inn, the Cardigan Arms, is named for the Earl of Cardigan who led the Light Brigade at Balaclava in 1854. Before that it was known as the Horse and Trumpet and the house was originally two cottages. Closed in the 1970s, it was the only pub in the village.

The Old Barn, Glooston, formerly the Blue Bell, in 1962.

The Fox and Goose Hotel, a well known landmark on Coalville's London Road, pictured in December 1961.

A February 1969 photograph of the White Hart in Harby.

In December 1962, builders working on renovations at the old Bewicke Arms inn at Hallaton discovered old newspapers and a life policy booklet dating back 100 years.

The Red Lion at Bottesford in December 1968.

Where People Gathered

Street corner meetings were popular during the first half of this century and the Suffragettes' platform was often the scene of noisy dispute and sometimes violence. This one in Leicester has certainly drawn a crowd.

Crowds in the Market Place for the Coronation Day Service on 22 June 1911.

A vast crowd in the Town Hall Square at a memorial service following the death of King George V in January 1936.

The three 'bottles' are held aloft to signal the start of the Hallaton Bottle Kicking, in April 1936.

A queue for coke at the Gas Works in February 1947. Some had waited since 3.15am to purchase half-hundredweights of coke in one of the worst winters in living memory.

Holidaymakers queue for trains to Skegness from Belgrave Road Station in August 1953. The passenger services were used for the last time in September 1962.

May 1955 and a crowd at De Montfort Hall Gardens variety entertainment, which included a performance by the Band of the Irish Guards.

Summer holidays may be over for these young ladies in August 1955, but the memories will linger on for many years. The queue is waiting to collect holiday snaps from the chemists.

A huge crowd queuing for FA Cup tickets in January 1956 at Leicester City's Filbert Street ground. After beating Luton 4-0 at Kenilworth Road, Leicester were drawn at home to Stoke City.

The City Transport's holiday attraction 'Leicester Tour' was as popular as ever. Large queues lined up in Charles Street to take their seats in August 1956.

Some of the queue in Albion Street, Leicester, on Valentine's Day in 1959, for 300 tickets to see the TV show *Oh Boy!* in London the following Saturday.

Coronation Street jammed Leicester's High Street on 21 April 1962. Mile-long lines of cars, lorries and buses were held up in and around the city centre after the arrival of Martha Longhurst, Minnie Caldwell and Annie Walker at a High Street store. Lines of stationary vehicles blocked Pocklington's Walk, Welford Road to beyond the Granby Halls, Southgate Street, Oxford Street and Woodgate.

Martha, Minnie and Annie – in real life Lynne Carol, Margot Bryant and Doris Speed – had left the Rovers' Return for the official reopening of a fancy goods shop. Over an hour before the stars arrived, their fans had flocked to High Street in their hundreds to make sure of getting a kerbside view of their favourites.

Crowds lining the pavement outside the Grand Hotel expecting to see world heavyweight boxing champion Sonny Liston. It took the appearance of a police patrol car and a police motor cyclist to convince them that there had been a change of plans.

Beatlemania gripped Leicester in October 1963 when huge queues waited to get tickets for a concert by the Beatles to be held at De Montfort Hall. The crowds in their thousands waited along Charles Street and Halford Street, until the booking office in the old Municipal Buildings opened. Suddenly there was a noise that sounded like a gun shot. It was in fact a large plate glass window on the Halford's Cycle shop cracking and starting to fall on to the vast throng below. Instantly a hand shot up and held the window until help arrived. Amazingly the glass didn't shatter and the area was made safe.

The Lord Mayor's Show of May 1964. Tens of thousands lined the route to see 100 floats and seven bands, seen here passing the Clock Tower and making their way up High Street.

A young girl fan shows her enthusiasm at the Monsters of Rock festival at Donington Park.

Loughborough Market Place in November 1970, transformed into a fairground for the annual three-day November Fair, which was ceremonially opened by the Deputy Mayor, Councillor the Revd J. N. L. Thompson. The street fair is held by permission of a charter signed by King Henry III in 1228.

A scene from one of Loughborough's many 1953 Coronation street parties. This one was in Regent Street and the picture was contributed by Mrs Agnes Pell, formerly of number 51A. Those homes, then decorated, have now all been demolished.

Happy faces round trestle tables in the gaily beflagged street – a scene that was soon to become commonplace all over Leicester. The picture was taken at one of the first Coronation street tea parties, held for the children of Windley Road and Elmwood Road, Saffron Lane estate in June 1953.

The Clock Tower forms the perfect setting – almost in period style – for the Lord Mayor's coach in procession in May 1964.

Memories... Billy Bates

HE was born in a converted bus, and though current 'winter quarters' are a spacious bungalow in Enderby, Leicestershire, it is still a mobile home.

"Oh yes, it's got to have wheels on it" smiles Billy Bates, the boss of Bates's Funfairs, as he surveys his latest funfair set-up at Victoria Park, Leicester.

Billy is a sixth generation fairground man, and his business is still a family affair.

"My son James looks after the dodgems, my son Kennedy does the waltzers, my wife does the catering and the books," he began, before reeling off a whole list of relations involved in the business.

"As for me, I was born on a fairground, and I never did give any other job any consideration."

Shy boy: Bill, aged three, on his tricycle. Behind him are prizes for the coconut shy.

Bus baby: Mum, Dad and baby Billy Bates, in front of the converted bus where he was born.

Billy's earliest memories are all tangled up with funfairs. He was born in 1946 on a Leyland Bus at Thrapston, Northamptonshire, which his Dad had converted into a caravan.

The bus towed a four-wheel trailer on the back, with all the equipment in. These days it's a lorry with the equipment in that tows the caravan.

"My first job was with my Grandad Bates on the coconut shy – three balls for sixpence and seven for a shilling. And in some places they chucked the ball at *you*, if they missed with the first two. I was five years old."

The family acquired a 16ft Eccles caravan. "The big new thing was Calor Gas," recalls Billy. "And the engineers fitted up two gas mantles on each side of the fireplace."

With the constant travelling, and no regular schooling, it was Billy's mother who taught him to read and write.

Next home was a 'fantastic' 22-foot Fairview caravan – "A big showman's caravan with rosebowl windows and polished mahogany all the way through, made by Brayshaws of Yeadon."

And in the meantime Billy was gaining more and more fairground experience, all over the country.

So what was the fairground attraction for this lifelong showman?

"I like the fresh air, the freedom – there's no clocking on or clocking off – and I like the welcome we get all over the place. It's a very social life, being a showman.

"If we go to Braunstone for instance, we use the same pubs as the locals, the same fish and chip shop, we're part of the community for the duration of the fair."

And is there any downside? "Doing all the hard work, and then it raining."

Billy reckons funfairs like his have changed subtly over the years. The physical challenges, like that coconut shy, have been replaced by ever-faster 'sit and be thrilled' rides.

The funfair is also safer and more family orientated than it used to be, and the prizes are better. But the thrill is still there.

"Over the years we've had more and more competition, from theme parks to television," Billy admits. "But a funfair's got that atmosphere.

"It's the music, the sound of the generators, the smell of the hot dogs. There's still nothing that really compares with it."

The next generation: Billy with his sons James (left) and Kennedy, the seventh generation of showmen.

Children dance round the maypole some time in the 1930s.

The opening of Victoria Park Lodges in the 1930s.

The crowd in the Grandstand at Abbey Park enjoying the 1932 Leicester Pageant.

A quaint touch is given by this clash of two centuries, made even more so by the fact that the car itself is a museum piece today.

The Earl of Leicester offers a lady of Tudor times a light for her cigarette!

Three pretty maids upon their horses wait to enter the arena for their scene.

A young lady taking part in the parade at the Leicester Mercury Historic Transport Pageant and Vehicle Parade, held every year in May since 1988.

This Sporting Life

Leicester Fosse Football Club was founded in 1884 and moved to the Filbert Street ground in 1891, changing their name to Leicester City in 1919. The club were League Cup winners in 1964 and FA Charity Shield winners in 1971. Their highest position in the top flight was second in the old Division One in 1929. Leicester City have been FA Cup Finalists four times – 1949, 1961, 1963 and 1969 – but they did not win at Wembley until 1994 when a 2-1 victory over Derby County in the First Division Play-offs gave them promotion to the Premier League. They were soon relegated but won back their place in 1996 with a 1-0 victory over Crystal Palace at Wembley. Famous Leicester City players include goalkeepers Gordon Banks (1959-67) and Peter Shilton (1965-74), and striker Gary Lineker (1977-85). John O'Neill is City's most capped player, appearing for Northern Ireland 39 times from 1976 to 1987. In 1996, Leicester won the Coca-Cola Cup, beating Middlesbrough in a replay 1-0 at Hillsborough after a 1-1 draw at Wembley.

Blue Army! Straw hats and flat caps were the order of the day for the Filbert Street crowd in the 1920s. Notice the separate press boxes.

Ace marksman Arthur Chandler (second left) in action for Leicester City between the wars.

Leicester City in 1925-26. Back row (left to right): Jarvie, Heathcock, Bamber, Viner, Campbell, Sharp, Keywood, Carrigan, Hooper, Godderidge. Middle row: Osborne, Black, Brown, Findlay, Watson, Newton, Baxter, Allan, Carr, Gibbs, Fox. Front row: King, Duncan (captain), Adcock, Hine, Chandler, Lochhead, Webb, Wadsworth, Hackett, Gouch, Gardner (trainer).

Don Revie (out of picture) scores the winning goal at Highbury when Leicester City beat Portsmouth 1-0 in the 1949 FA Cup semi-final.

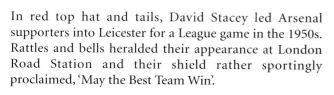

Leicester City's 1949 FA Cup squad, complete with autographs. They lost 3-1 to Wolves in the Final.

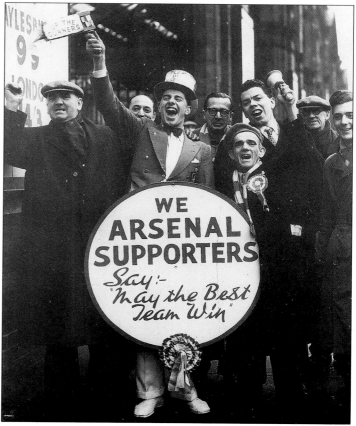

In red top hat and tails, David Stacey led Arsenal supporters into Leicester for a League game in the 1950s. Rattles and bells heralded their appearance at London Road Station and their shield rather sportingly proclaimed, 'May the Best Team Win'.

Memories... Arthur Rowley

THERE are probably retired goalkeepers all over Britain who still wake up in a sweat as Arthur Rowley rampages through their dreams.

Arthur was the goalkeeper's worst nightmare, 'The Gunner' who bulldozed defences and bulged the net with a ripsnorting left.

In a Leicester City career that stretched from 1950 to 1958, Rowley notched a club record 256 goals in 319 games.

"There's no secret to it," says the reserved Rowley, now in his 70s, speaking from his modest Shropshire home. "You just get into the right place at the right time.

"Of course you've got to be given the ball to score, and then I suppose I always said if you get six on target, one'll go in."

The statistics speak for themselves. For example, if you went to Filbert Street to see Rowley play for City, you had a 65 per cent chance of seeing him score at least one goal. And it was all achieved on a wage of between £12 and £14 a week.

"There wasn't a lot of money in the game then," Arthur sighed. "And I think the modern money is one of the things that spoilt the game."

What else has changed? Well, training for a start. Training back in the 1950s was pretty basic. "Just running round the track, not much ball skill involved and not much coaching either," recalls Arthur.

Refereeing has changed too. "You've only got to cough near a referee these days, and you'll be booked."

Arthur Rowley wheels away arm outstretched, goalkeeper grounded, after notching another goal in the 1955-56 campaign.

"In my day you didn't look to the referee if you got fouled, you just used to get up, dust yourself off, and think, 'it's you turn next son'."

Arthur's best season for City was 1956-57, when the club was promoted to Division One – the old top flight. He scored an astonishing 44 goals in 43 games.

He never played for his country though. City yo-yoed up and down the divisions in the 1950s and according to Arthur, "If you didn't play for certain leading clubs, you didn't play for England".

Then in 1958, his City career came to abrupt halt. He had just enjoyed a decent season in Division One despite an ankle injury – 20 goals in 26 games.

"But someone in the club – I won't say who – wanted me out. I suppose they thought I was past my best. It came as a shock. Yes, I was bitter at the time."

More fool the Leicester City bosses. Happily, Arthur had the last word.

He went on to score more than 150 goals in 236 games for Shrewsbury Town, to become a football legend in that town too.

And he has recently been named by the Football League as one of the 100 Football League Legends, to coincide with the League's own 100th anniversary.

And why? Because those Shrewsbury goals, added to his Leicester tally, helped make Arthur

Welcome back. An emotional Arthur Rowley gets a huge ovation from City supporters on a recent return to Filbert Street.

the Football League's all-time leading scorer, with 434 League goals in 619 games.

It's a record that half a century later still hasn't been broken.

The class of '57 – Arthur with the team that had just been promoted to the old First Division. He is the one with the ball, to the right of the shield.

Leicester City in 1959-60 when their manager was Matt Gillies (in suit, front row). Seated behind him is future England goalkeeper Gordon Banks.

Action from the FA Cup semi-final between Leicester City and West Bromwich Albion at Hillsborough on 29 March 1969. Peter Shilton clears an Albion attack aided by Allan Clarke and Graham Cross with Albion's John Talbut the odd man out.

The old Main Stand at Filbert Street.

The Leicester City crowd during Jimmy Bloomfield's era. The banner at the front refers to the time four City players – Shilton, Worthington, Weller and Whitworth – were current England internationals.

Keith Weller here seen beating Peter Storey to score his second goal in a 4-1 win against Arsenal on 23 October 1976.

Frank Worthington, a great City favourite, seen here in August 1977 playing against Coventry City.

Gary Lineker was born in Leicester on 30 November 1960. A natural goalscorer, he netted 103 in 209 appearances for City between July 1977 and June 1985. Here he is being congratulated by Steve Lynex in May 1985 after adding one to that tally.

Steve Walsh scores the winning goal against Derby County at Wembley in the 1994 Division One Play-off Final.

Goalscorer Steve Claridge holds up the Coca-Cola Cup. City beat Middlesbrough 1-0 to win the trophy after a replay in 1996.

An extremely interesting view of Victoria Park pavilion with an unknown cricket team gracing the foreground at the end of the last century.

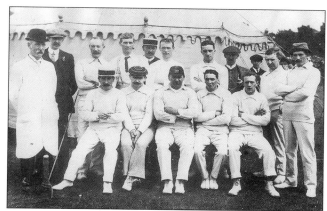

A local cricket team pictured at Victoria Park before a game to mark the Coronation of George V in June 1911.

Cricket on Victoria Park just after World War Two. Nissen huts can be seen around the edge of the park. Perhaps they were changing rooms for the sportsmen and women as the pavilion had been destroyed by a mine during the war.

The trophy's ours – Ray Illingworth holds aloft the Benson & Hedges Cup after a magnificent five-wicket win over Middlesex in the Final at Lords in July 1975. Leicestershire County Cricket Club was formed in 1879 and gained first-class status in 1894. They played at Grace Road in Leicester from 1894 to 1900, then used a ground in Aylestone Road between 1901 and 1939, but moved back to Grace Road in 1946. Honours include the County Championship in 1975 and 1996, and the Sunday League Championship in 1974 and 1977. Leicestershire were also Benson & Hedges Cup winners in 1972, 1975 and 1985, and NatWest Trophy runners-up in 1992. Some of their most famous names were Harold 'Dickie' Bird (1960-64), Ray Illingworth (1969-78), Leicestershire's most capped player David Gower (1975-89) and Jonathan Agnew (1978-90).

A youthful David Gower glancing one down the leg-side for Leicestershire.

The 1996 Britannic Assurance County Champions Trophy with Phil Simmons and James Whitaker, the county captain.

Leicester Football Club was formed in 1880 and played at the Belgrave Cricket and Cycle Ground or Victoria Park. Their first opponents were Moseley and the game was drawn. Leicester moved to Welford Road in 1892 and soon acquired the nickname 'Tigers', probably as a result of changing from all-black to chocolate and yellow colours. The letters A to G were used on the forwards' shirts from 1926 and lettering extended to the whole team by 1931. By this time the red, green and white strip was in use. Leicester won the first National Courage League Division One Championship in 1988 and again in 1995. Victory in the John Player Cup came in three successive seasons – 1979, 1980 and 1981. The 1993 Pilkington Cup Final resulted in a 23-16 victory for Tigers over Harlequins. Famous past players include Peter Wheeler (1969-85), Dusty Hare (1976-89), Les Cusworth (1978-90) and Martin Johnson is one of the stars of today. The Alliance & Leicester Stand, completed in 1995, has made Welford Road the best Rugby Union ground in England after Twickenham.

Gotcha! Rory Underwood is caught trying to break through the Bristol defence in April 1985.

Paul Dodge, centre.

Les Cusworth, fly half.

Pete Wheeler, hooker.

Dusty Hare, full-back.

Tigers v The Barbarians in December 1976, a traditional Christmas fixture. Back row (left to right): Chalkie White (coach), Steve Johnson (replacement), John Duggan, Garry Adey, Brian Hall, Dave Forfar, Nick Joyce, Jim Kempin, Bob Barker, Robin Cowling, Peter Wheeler, Paul Dodge. Front row: Dusty Hare, Larry Parkes (replacement), Bleddyn Jones, Bob Rowell, Steve Kenney, Jez Krych.

Tigers' magnificent six (left to right): Dusty Hare, Nick Youngs, Peter Wheeler, Les Cusworth, Paul Dodge and Clive Woodward, all picked to play for England in November 1983.

Grim determination on Dean 'Deano' Richards' face during a Tigers match against Blackheath in December 1984.

The Grandstand entrance to Leicester Stadium on Blackbird Road, home of speedway, stock car racing and greyhounds, seen here in 1960.

Leicester Lions speedway team line up as they prepared for the first home match against Coventry in 1973. The absentee is skipper Ray Wilson. From left to right: Norman Storer, John Boulger, Malcolm Shakespeare, Dave Jessup, Malcolm Brown and Brian Foote.

Stock car racing and speedway were popular spectator sports at Blackbird Road. Here we see some daredevil drivers thrilling the crowds in May 1953.

Willie Thorne, seen here with Steve Davis and the 'Dulux dog'. Thorne was born in Leicester and began his professional snooker career in 1974. The highlight was winning the Mercantile Credit Classic at Warrington in 1985, but he has been successful in at least two dozen other tournaments. In 1981 the Willie Thorne Snooker Club was established in Charles Street, Leicester. This family business now has a membership of over 5,400 and is regarded as the top club in the country for the number of tournaments held.

Boxing, both amateur and professional, has been a popular sport in Leicester for many years. Venues have ranged from working men's clubs and Cossington Street Swimming Baths to Tigers' Football Ground and Granby Halls. Several local boxers have progressed in the sport. Leicester's Chris Pyatt became a World middleweight champion and both Jack Gardner, a heavyweight from Market Harborough, and Tony Sibson, a middleweight from Leicester (*pictured*) became British champions.

George Aldridge was a British middleweight, Tony McKenzie a British light-welterweight and Tim Wood a light-heavyweight champion.

Joe Jacobs, landlord of the Haunch of Venison in High Street, Leicester, promoted numerous local events at Granby Halls. He was second only to Jack Solomons, the famous London promoter, as an arranger of top international boxing matches in this country.

Chris Pyatt, who became a World middleweight champion, to add to his British and European light-middleweight triumphs.

Sebastian Coe studied economics and social history at Loughborough University. From 1981 to 1984 he was a research assistant. During this period he won gold for the 1,500 metres and silver in the 800 metres at the 1980 Moscow Olympics. In 1981 he set world records for the 800, 1,000 metres and mile, and at the Los Angeles Olympics of 1984 he won gold for the 1,500 metres and silver for the 800 metres again, retaining the 1,500 title which has never been achieved before.

This is a picture athletics fans thought they may never see as deadly rivals Steve Ovett (left) and Sebastian Coe share a joke at Loughborough University athletics track. The pair met, off the track, during the match between Loughborough Students Past and Present and the AAAs.

In 1979 the only racehorse to have an official fan club was born at Ab Kettleby. Desert Orchid won the Cheltenham Gold Cup in 1989 and his trainer was inundated with letters. Other horses were in danger of being neglected so the fan club was set up to answer the mail. Desert Orchid has come first in 34 races including four King George V Chases, the Irish Grand National and the Whitbread Gold Cup. His popularity stemmed partly from his grey colour, but also from the fact that he loved attention and always looked straight at the camera. Newly-retired Desert Orchid receives a pat from Mrs Midge Burridge at the Ab Kettleby stables in January 1992.

Leicester played host to the World Cycle Championships in the summer of 1970, held at the Sports Centre on Saffron Lane.

Ice skaters at the Leicester Boulevard rink pictured about 1910.

Members of Spinney Park Bowls Club measure up during a match in the 1900s.

Entertaining Leicester

This photograph, taken outside the old Picture House cinema on Granby Street early in the summer of 1943, recalls a film which must have guaranteed a full house at every performance. Its theme was the Battle of Britain and it was shown as part of a special War Week event in Leicester.

The Tudor Cinema on Vaughan Street in June 1958. It was soon to close as television became the number one entertainment.

The twin-domed Evington Cinema on East Park Road on fire in November 1984. The cinema had opened in 1916 and the last films were seen on its screen in 1978. The fire destroyed the roof but the frontage and walls were saved.

Built in the late 1930s, the Odeon, on the corner of Rutland Street and Queen Street, was probably Leicester's most impressive cinema. With its Art Deco modern look it was a particular favourite with city folk. The death knell sounded in 1997 since when it has remained unused.

The Plaza Cinema in Whetstone in March 1959.

Pictured in October 1960, Kibworth's privately-owned village hall. Villagers were to decide at a public meeting whether or not to buy it. It served as both cinema and dance hall.

The Ritz Cinema in South Wigston about 1941.

The Oadby Cinema, seen here in June 1972. Showing at the time was *Kelly's Heroes* starring Clint Eastwood.

The spectacular Throne Room scene in Prince Littler's pantomime *The Sleeping Beauty* at the Opera House at Christmas 1950.

The Theatre Royal on Horsefair Street which opened in 1836 opposite Bowling Green Street, pictured in February 1957.

A queue outside the Palace Theatre at 5.30pm on Friday, 27 June 1947.

Memories... Sir Richard Attenborough

Scouting days – Richard Attenborough (centre) in his days with the 9th Leicester Boy Scouts.

"RICHARD, do you think you can act?" It was the early 1930s, and young Richard Attenborough had two days to learn his lines, after a fellow scout in the 9th Leicester troop fell ill.

It turned out that the lad could act a bit. In fact, he seemed to enjoy it.

An idea formed in his mind, sharpened when his father – the Principal of Leicester University College as it was then – took 11-year-old Richard to see Charlie Chaplin in *The Gold Rush.*

"If any one thing persuaded me to become an actor, it was seeing Chaplin in that film," recalls Lord Attenborough. "It was magical."

So by 1935, a 12-year-old Richard was putting on his own show – at St Barnabas Hall in North Evington, Leicester.

"To raise the ten shilling hire fee, I bought dozens of little notepads for a penny each, the same number of pencils for less than a penny each, and tied them together with a piece of coloured string," remembers Lord Attenborough.

"Then I sold them to friends at Wyggeston School in Leicester for threepence each."

He even persuaded younger brother David, later to become a TV naturalist, to appear in one sketch. David agreed, providing all the profits were donated to the RSPCA!

And at last Mr Attenborough senior managed to swallow the disappointment that Richard was not destined for great things academically.

After the St Barnabas show, he told his wife, "We had better let Dickie do what he wants to do."

Richard went to the Royal Academy of Dramatic Art, and by 1946 was a worldwide film star, his most famous role probably Pinkie in the film *Brighton Rock.*

In 1948 he returned to Leicester to star in the stage play *Home of the Brave,* at the Leicester Opera House.

Sir Richard Attenborough in Leicester at the launch of a building fund appeal for the Centre for Disability and the Arts.

That building was demolished in 1960, and replaced by the Malcolm Arcade. It is one of four major Leicester theatres that have gone – the others were the Theatre Royal in Horsefair Street, the Prince of Wales in Belgrave Gate and the Palace Theatre of Varieties, also in Belgrave Gate.

Richard was part of the original cast in Agatha Christie's play *The Mousetrap,* and was an award winner in the film *Seance on a Wet Afternoon.*

And he made his debut as a film director in 1968, with the musical *Oh! What A Lovely War.*

But his biggest cinema triumph was the film *Gandhi,* in 1982, which he directed.

He said it took him 20 years to bring the project to fruition. "But I never lost heart. I had absolute confidence that somehow, some day, it would happen."

Now in his 70s, Richard Attenborough still leads the British film industry from the front.

"Yes, I do feel a responsibility beyond my own work," he says "It's a load to carry, because I tend to be leading the charge."

But he still hasn't forgotten his Leicester roots. He is the hard-working patron of the Centre for Disability and the Arts in Leicester, the city he still calls home.

Sir Richard Attenborough watches students at work in the Centre for Disability and the Arts, of which he is patron.

The music hall days are over and Leicester's Palace Theatre was reduced to showing 'Art Films' as the posters tell us. It finally closed its doors in March 1957. At one time Leicester was only second to London for variety shows.

Girls dancing the night away at a Leicester night spot.

Rock 'n Rollers jiving to the beat of the 1950s music.

July 1964 and screaming girls mob the taxi as the Rolling Stones leave the De Montfort Hall, Leicester, after their show. One girl is seen hanging from the luggage rack as the car moved off.

Memories... Showaddywaddy

An early publicity photograph.

Best-ever concert? Showaddywaddy at a packed De Montfort Hall, Leicester in October 1976.

THE time was October 1976, the place was a packed De Montfort Hall, Leicester, and the event was billed as 'The Greatest Rock 'n' Roll Show Ever'.

An outrageous boast of course, but there were few people in this home crowd likely to sue the eight Leicester lads who made up rock band Showaddywaddy.

After all, the city band were on a run of ten Top Ten hits, and had just celebrated a number one – *Under The Moon Of Love*.

So as lead singer Dave Bartram adjusted his shades, bellowed, "It's great to be back," at the crowd and launched into a series of no-nonsense hits, people danced in the cramped spaces in front of their seats and roared back their approval.

The next day's *Leicester Mercury* duly recorded 'fans going wild with delight'.

Dave, now in his mid-40s and living in Rutland, recalls it as the best concert of the band's career.

Showaddywaddy was formed in 1973 from two four-man groups doing the rounds of pubs and clubs in Leicestershire – The Hammers and The Choice. They kept all eight members, and went from strength to strength.

Dave vividly remembers the first appearance on *Top of the Pops*.

"There was some sort of technicians' strike, so we ended up playing on a Morecambe and Wise set, in front of a couple of settees."

The band's career really took off when they did a cover version of *Three Steps To Heaven* in 1975. ("The formula for heaven's very simple, wop wah-ooh.")

And their canny revival of *Under The Moon of Love* the next year sold almost a million copies.

The kind critics said, "They present a fully-fledged, no-holds-barred, all-out rock and roll show. And they play it pretty well too."

The unkind ones said, "They do nothing new."

Today Dave will freely admit, "The cover versions were so successful that our label stuck us to a tried and tested formula.

"We were so busy touring and gigging, we didn't notice. Yes, we stuck to the formula for too long."

Still, the 'hardest-working band in the world' had about seven years at the very top, kept their feet on the ground, and avoided the worst excesses of the notorious music business.

So what are Showaddywaddy doing now, 20 years on?

Pointing at his hairline, a youthful Dave will admit to 'a bit of a recession', but he proudly says, "We still play literally everywhere ...One night in front of 20,000 people in Berlin, the next for a few hundred Hoorah Henrys in a marquee."

As well as Dave, at the last count there were four more of the original band members still clinging to the bandwagon.

"We're not exactly broke, but we're not exactly well off either," admits Dave.

"But even if we could, I don't think we would give up playing. We still get a buzz from going on stage."

So when will the band call it a day? "We reckon New Year's Eve, 1999," laughs Dave. "But who knows? We may keep coming back!"

Still going strong. Dave Bartram (right) in his rehearsal room in Corby, gets ready for another tour.

Some Famous Faces

A group photographed on the occasion of the visit of King Edward VII and Queen Alexandra to Gopsall Hall in 1908. The King and Queen are standing, towards the centre of the back row. Earl Howe is seated in the centre and the two figures on the extreme left in the back line bear a striking resemblance to the Kaiser and his son, the Crown Prince William. However, a record of their having visited Gopsall has not been confirmed.

William Buckler's factory in Walnut Street – alas no more – waiting for the Prince of Wales (later Edward VIII and then the Duke of Windsor) to unveil a plaque at the Liberty Shoe Works in the early 1930s. But the route was changed and the Royal party went down Jarrom Street instead.

The Duke of York, later to become King George VI, unveiling the war memorial in The Square, Countesthorpe. Later the memorial was removed to its present home in the Churchyard to make way for a traffic roundabout.

Royal visit to the city, October 1946. King George VI and Queen Elizabeth accompanied by the Lord Mayor (Alderman Worthington) and his wife the Lady Mayoress.

The Queen with Mr R. L. Wessel on a Royal visit to Leicester in May 1958.

Stage and radio singer Adelaide Hall tries her hand at shoe machining, watched by an audience of experts, at the factory of P. W. Shoes Ltd, Anstey, in February 1948. Miss Hall was staying with her friend, Mrs T. H. Stanley of Leicester Road, Rearsby.

Memories… Jennifer Lewis

Moment of truth: Jennifer Lewis on parade in the Miss World contest in 1967.

Jennifer today: Now Mrs Bryers, and living in Australia, and would you believe 50 this year!

SHE may sound like an ordinary Australian housewife now, but Jennifer Bryers has two secrets.

Number one – she's not Australian. In fact, she's from Glenfield in Leicestershire.

Number two – as Jennifer Lewis she was a Miss England, a Miss UK and a finalist in Miss World and Miss Universe.

"Ow, the Lister Mercury!" she

On the phone to Mum before the Miss UK competition in 1966.

twanged, genuinely pleased, when the paper tracked her down to her latest home in Buderim, a 'touristy' area on the east coast of Australia, not too far from Darwin.

"It's wonderful to hear from you. I still feel a great affection for Leicester and the people who live there. Tell everyone back home I really wish

them the very best, I pray for them, and I'm coming back one day!"

Think back if you can to 1967, the year of the Pill, Flower Power, Che Guevera, Donald Campbell and *Sergeant Pepper's Lonely Hearts Club Band*.

It was in that year that the unarguably lovely Miss Lewis, then aged 20, became Leicester's finest contribution to the swinging 60s, by winning or reaching the final of …every beauty contest going.

Her professionalism knew no bounds.

"For the last two nights I have slept on my front with my head on my arms to avoid crushing my hair," she told the *Mercury* after the televised Miss UK contest.

And she was never bland with the quotes either. Asked what she would do with one lot of prize money, she replied, "Put it all on the floor and roll in it."

For a year her face and her figure were everywhere, from TV shows to local garage openings.

And there are no regrets about her career. "I was very fortunate in life to have that early success," said Mrs Bryers today. "I wouldn't have missed it, and I'm grateful for it. It gave me so much experience of life at a very young age, and took me right round the world."

But the next year someone else got voted in, of course, Jenny became ex-Miss UK, and nobody wanted last year's model.

"Initially, there was a big feeling of anti-climax, a period of adjustment," she admitted. "But then other things crop up".

She married Australian Ian Bryers in 1978, and moved out to Australia a year later.

She still lives with Ian, who manages 'one of the largest motels in Australia', plus son Joseph, aged nine, at a house near the coast with about one-and-a-half acres of land.

She still does some modelling, and self-deprecatingly says, "We older girls are still in demand." She's 50 now, and still looking good.

"I would really love to tell you about my fitness regime. but the truth is I don't have time to do much – just occasional water aerobics."

But she claims to still miss Leicester, from St Barnabas Primary School and the market, to Humberstone Park, and people calling her 'm'duck'.

So any regrets about her long-distance move?

"I can't regret anything – no, no. I think things have turned out pretty much as they were meant to be."

Pictured at the Home Life Exhibition held at the Granby Halls in September 1972, is Michael Parkinson chatting to two girls from a local builder's stand.

Stars of the De Montfort Hall pantomime, *Cinderella*. Leicester's very own Bill Maynard, who plays the Baron, is at the keyboard, accompanied by (left to right) Jessica Martin (Cinderella), Patrick Mower (Prince Charming), Peggy Mount (Fairy Godmother) and producer Freddie Davies. Bill Maynard worked in the city when he left school and was on Leicester City's books before launching his showbusiness career.

Rosemary Conley launched her diet and fitness clubs based at Quorn in 1993 and there are now over 2,000 weekly classes throughout the UK. For 25 years she has run her fitness and slimming business from Leicestershire. Her *Hip and Thigh Diet,* first published in 1988, together with the sequel and other books and videos, have sold over 6 million to date.

Sue Townsend who had phenomenal success with her novel *The Secret Diary of Adrian Mole aged 13½.*

First priority: Geoff Hamilton, the BBC TV garden expert from *Gardeners' World*, pictured in the garden of his home at Barnsdale. With an already crowded schedule, he refused to take on any extra commitments if they threatened to curtail the amount of time he spent at work there.

Arnold George Dorsey was born in Madras in 1936 and came to Leicestershire when his family returned from India in 1947. Gerry Dorsey remained relatively obscure but as Englebert Humperdink he had a 1967 hit with *Release Me* followed immediately by *The Last Waltz* and *Man Without Love* . Over the next six years there were another 11 chart hits. Englebert now lives in America but still has a family home in Great Glen. Here he joins in a game of Scrabble at LOROS Day Centre in Ratcliffe Road, Stoneygate in December 1984.

Sir Frank Whittle, who developed the jet engine during World War Two, seen here after signing three copies of his book for winners of a children's poster competition in June 1987. The lucky recipients were Ian Richardson (10) of Wycliffe County Primary School, Lutterworth, Claire Belcher (10) of the Sherrier Primary School, Lutterworth, and Simon Reed (14) of Lutterworth High School.

Funny Old World

Leicester's Pearly King and Queen, Mr and Mrs Bill White, with their donkey cart, before the start of the Coronation parade through Leicester to the Newarke Houses.

Mr Jack Cox, Knowle Farm, Thurlaston, lights up his pipe at the sale of the wether at the Nag's Head, Enderby, on Whit Monday in May 1969. On the left is Mr B. Woolman of 19 Federation Street, Enderby, the purchaser of the wether.

Meat shortages are illustrated here at a butcher's shop on Narborough Road when Mr Owen Williams chalked up this message in February 1951.

The traditional ceremony of putting the pig on the wall to watch the band go by at a pre-war carnival. The wall, facing The Square, Countesthorpe, belonged to Mr Cosby, a farmer in the village.

'This one has got to come out ...!" At least that's what this workman with the pliers appears to be saying, but it's not an extraction he has in mind. Mr Roy Ingram is actually tightening up a valve in the mouth of one of the Leicester Town Hall Square wyverns so that, along with its companions, it can spray water again for the first time in six years, in 1976.

A notice outside Kibworth Cemetery in January 1970.

Leicester's blizzard of 28 March 1916. Here is a picture taken then by Mr F. Lumbers of 157 Upperton Road, Leicester. How different Saffron Lane looks today.

The winter of 1947 was a cruel one and this photograph shows a road near Tilton after German and Italian prisoners-of-war had cleared a way through.

A snow-covered New Walk in January 1960.

A heavy fog in Gallowtree Gate in January 1964, similar to the smog of the 1940s and 1950s. A few shoppers brave the elements as a bus with headlights on full slowly makes its way out of town.

This was the churned-up ground adjoining the Lee Street car park. Shopkeepers had complained that drivers used the waste ground instead of the official park. The picture was taken shortly after a heavy lorry had been towed out after being bogged down to its axle in January 1954.

A flooded Fosse Road North in the late 1960s.

Dennis Buckley's picture of Spinney Hill Park in November 1954 was one of the exhibits put on view by Imperial Typewriters' Art and Photographic Club. Dennis waited for two years to get the correct lighting effect for another of his exhibits.

Autumn mist and the sun filtering through beech leaves lend enchantment to this picture of an urban oasis ... 'one of the oldest parts of Leicester, which has so far happily stood firm against the creeping tide of concrete'. The photograph shows the graceful spire of St Mary de Castro viewed from riverside Castle Gardens in October 1970.

A misty New Walk at King Street in winter with the sun just breaking through.

Memories… of Graham Chapman

"The worst case of party pooping I've ever seen." That was how a devastated, but still quipping, Terry Jones described the death of Leicestershire's major contribution to TV comedy.

The comic genius was Graham Chapman, and he had died of cancer on the day before a party planned to celebrate the 21st anniversary of the show he co-founded in 1968 – *Monty Python's Flying Circus*.

Graham poses with most of the team just two months before his death. Left to right Terry Gilliam, John Cleese, Terry Jones, Graham and Michael Palin.

Genial madman – Monty Python co-founder Graham Chapman.

"We all knew Graham came from Leicester," said Terry Jones, "But as far as I was concerned he had come from the moon."

In fact Graham came from a very respectable county background. His father was a former police chief inspector at Melton. His brother became a leading consultant at Northampton General Hospital.

Graham was educated in Wigston, Melton Grammar School, and Cambridge University. He was supposed to have been a doctor himself. But at university he was lured into comedy writing, and went on to contribute to 1960s shows like *At Last the 1948 Show*, *The Frost Report*, *I'm Sorry I'll Read That Again* and *Marty*.

Why comedy, not medicine? "Less effort, more fun" he admitted once.

But Graham shot to worldwide fame, when he founded *Monty Python* with John Cleese, Michael Palin, Eric Idle, Terry Jones and Terry Gilliam.

He wrote some of the show's best-remembered sketches, from The Ministry of Silly Walks featuring a rubber-legged Cleese, to the Parrot Sketch, featuring a dead 'Norwegian Blue' parrot.

Plum parts in the sketches seldom went to laid-back Graham though. He smiled and shrugged as the others vied for the funny lines.

"I did most of my writing with John Cleese," he recalled. "Our habit was to work together either out of my own house or his.

"I'd usually arrive about 10 o'clock in the morning, although I was usually late, even when we met at my own house.

"We'd sit there and drink endless cups of coffee, chat about the news, do the crosswords, read the newspapers – anything to put off that truly awful moment of actually having to write something funny down on paper."

The results of this long-winded process was mixed with contributions from the Palin-Jones team, Eric Idle who mainly wrote solo, and Terry Gilliam's barmy animations.

And why was it called *Monty Python's Flying Circus*? The BBC wanted a title in a hurry. The Head of Comedy suggested circus, someone added flying, and someone else suggested Monty Python, because he sounded like a bad theatrical agent.

"None of us liked it, but none of us hated it. Typical committee decision."

The team also made four films – *And Now For Something Completely Different*, *Monty Python and the Holy Grail*, *Life of Brian* and *Meaning of Life*.

Graham died in Maidstone General Hospital in October 1989. He was 48.

Jim Yoakum, author of a Chapman biography/scrapbook called *Graham Crackers*, summed up: "He was an immensely talented under-achiever, with virtually no ego, and a mad glint in his eye."

Oi! that bin's for rubbish not for snoozing in! But he can't hear, poor chap, he's sound asleep. Perhaps he wouldn't mind if you put your old cigarette packets in his pocket. A picture taken in Charles Street, Leicester, in October 1978.

Life has not been kind to this old boy, but he makes the best of it!

A gentleman of the road in August 1961.

Sloped geometrically across a splintered trestle table with an uncompromising wooden post nestling in the small of the back doesn't make for the average conception of comfortable sleeping. But necessity is also the master of adaptation as well as the mother of invention, and the shelter of the Leicester Market is sufficient for a tired old man.

He may be basking in a heatwave but, as far as John Massey is concerned, the weather – like life – is still rum. John with his distinctive woolly hat and a sequence of discarded cases, had been trudging up and down the Uppingham Road, Leicester, for more than two decades. When he was in the mood to be sociable he would try to strike up a conversation with his favourite opening gambit, "Rum weather today". The line was so familiar that it became his nickname.

Rural Reflections

Bridge Street, Loughborough in the 1920s.

The doomed buildings of the Market Place, Loughborough in 1927, shortly before demolition began. The large symmetrical range of buildings facing, ie from Hepworths to Martin, had been erected soon after 1700, and at that time must have been a very imposing block. Even at the period of their demolition, and after years of neglect, they still retained some of their original beauty, even a measure of grandeur.

Upper Castle Street, Hinckley, in 1934.

Mountsorrel Lock pictured at the turn of the century.

The canal bridge at Blaby, which was demolished in 1935.

The inclined plane at Foxton Locks, one of the most sophisticated pieces of apparatus ever constructed on English canals and an amazing feat of Victorian engineering, undergoes its annual spring clean.

The Three Swans Hotel sign looks down on the old Town Hall in Market Harborough on a February day in 1968.

Nottingham Street, Melton Mowbray, just before World War One.

Oakham Market Place in 1913.

There is real period flavour to this street view of Oakham. Believed to have been taken in the mid-1930s, it shows the Britannia Inn and R. & H. Chambers motorcycle engineers.

A bird's-eye view in April 1964 of London Road from the roof of St Peter's Church, Oadby. The position offers a wonderful panoramic view over a wide area.

A horse pulling a small cart waits for its owner in Desford in July 1950. Maybe he's having a pint in the Blacksmith's Arms.

Regent Street, Lutterworth on a sunny day in 1911.

Mountsorrel in December 1961.

Bird's-eye view in June 1964 of 'old' Coalville from a *Mercury* cameraman located on the Clock Tower War Memorial.

Leicester Road, Kibworth, in the late 1920s.

Anstey village centre in January 1964.

In February 1965, when Cropston Reservoir was drained for the big clean-up, there emerged a reminder of past hunting days in Bradgate Park – the ruins of the head gamekeeper's house. Pictured here before 1870, the once magnificent building, with stabling and kennels, has been under water for more than 90 years. From the house were organised the shoots of the Earl of Stamford and Warrington, who then lived at Bradgate.

The Square at Oakthorpe in May 1964.

Cosby village in September 1956.

In February 1960 the *Mercury* said: 'Charming thatched cottages standing at the corner of Birstall Road and Church Hill, the last vestiges of old Birstall …a reminder that Birstall was a village, in the full sense of the word, not so long ago.'

Ruins of Ashby Castle, seen here in 1967.

Kirby Muxloe Castle ruins showing the moat, bridge and gateway, which has a four-centred arch. The west tower gives an indication of what was intended to be the finish of upper walls.

These children pictured in Medbourne in 1906 seem to be dressed in their Sunday best, probably to go to Sunday School or on an outing.

A farmer leads his horse through Little Stretton in August 1954.

In Market Overton, this was once the school and the names of some old pupils are on the walls. It was then two flats; one occupied by Flight Lieutenant Edmunds of Wittering and the other by Flight Lieutenant Dopson of Cottesmore, in August 1958.

Three children sit in the Square at Hathern watching the cows go by in September 1950. In one of Hathern's thatched cottages once lived John Heathcoat, 20-year-old inventor of the labour-saving bobbinet machine which revolutionised the lace making industry more than a century earlier. When he and his Hathern bride established themselves in Loughborough, Luddites wrecked 55 of his frames and he moved to Tiverton.

Milking cows meander up the bridle road to a pasture field bathed in late summer sunshine in 1954 in the Leicestershire industrial village of Fleckney – but round those cows raged a controversy because of the mud they deposited on the footpath.

A view of Old Evington, possibly at the turn of the century.

Church Street, Lutterworth, in the 1930s.

Home from the harvest fields – a tractor drives through Lowesby village in August 1951.

Knipton village pump in September 1957.

In October 1960, a landmark on the road to Kirby, one of the two gate lodges of The Towers. The embattled style was intended to match the character of Kirby Castle. The Towers was then a Leicester City Welfare Department home for elderly men.

Measham High Street in August 1958 was on the main road from Nottingham to London.

The Stone Row, Moira, built in 1816, seen here in October 1957.

This picture of Braunstone was taken by Mr S. Dingley, and since he died in 1903 when in his 80s, the picture must have been taken around a century ago. This path turned off Braunstone Lane and was a favourite walk of Leicester people going through the village towards Hinckley Road.

Newtown Linford village about 1916.

Broughton Astley brook in June 1963.

A peaceful Burton Overy, seen here in September 1949.

Part of Cadeby village in April 1957.

The old mill at Caldecott has seen many changes through the ages. It was used as a garage in July 1961.

Memories… Ethel Alam

Happy together: Sardar and Ethel (second left) boating on the River Soar at Aylestone in the early 1930s.

FOR much of this century, Leicestershire has been a melting pot county.

Since at least the 1950s, people have arrived here from the Caribbean, from Asia and from Africa.

Will the different nationalities ever mix completely? Well, one county couple who showed the way, and defied the times, are Sardar and Ethel Alam.

Sardar was a Muslim, born in the Punjab in India to a family of herbal eye specialists.

Ethel was Church of England, born and bred in Leicester. Her father worked as a paving slab foreman for Leicester Council.

But when Sardar met Ethel in Wigston in 1929, love found a way through race, religion, and almost universal disapproval.

Sardar had come to Leicester to be educated, and found himself the only Asian schoolboy at Wigston Grammar School – and perhaps in Leicestershire.

"People were most friendly," he insisted. "No there was no racial prejudice at school, why should there be? There was no one to hit, only me!"

But marriage to an English girl – that was a different thing altogether.

Sardar met Ethel as he walked to school and she walked to work, and they both claimed 'good looks' attracted them to each other straightaway.

"And then we just seemed to keep meeting," said Ethel. "And it didn't seem to matter, where one of us went, the other was there. It seemed like destiny."

They decided to get married in 1932. They slipped away for a ceremony at a mosque in London. Ethel said: "We took my sister with us. But even she thought we were just going to have a day out in London."

Both sets of parents were furious. "Family and friends – there was nobody that would agree," said Ethel. "Everyone said 'it won't last'".

"My parents didn't like it either," said Sardar. "They sent me here for my education, and I got married instead."

It was the couple's three children that brought the families back on board. Through the years there were also grandchildren and great-grandchildren.

Sardar started a wholesale hosiery business, and then ran a market stall selling hosiery and knitwear. He did not retire until he was 75.

"I worked hard enough," said Sardar. "And we managed to make a decent life for ourselves." Ethel added: "We just pulled together. We managed."

And their different religions? "We never really bothered about it," said Ethel. "Like all these things, it's only a problem if you make it a problem, isn't it?

"I suppose we ignored all the rules and regulations. But we found nothing really matters if you get on well together."

And the marriage that everyone said wouldn't last, in fact lasted for 66 happy years.

"No we've got no great advice for couples like us," said the trailblazing Alams. "They've got to find that out for themselves."

Sardar died suddenly last year, aged 88. "Oh, I do miss him," said Ethel. "It was such a shock."

Ethel carried out his wishes for him to be buried as a Muslim. And when she went to the funeral at Saffron Hill, Leicester, it was only her second visit to a mosque.

Happy memories: Sardar and Ethel Alam at their home in Wigston.

A view of Castle Donington taken from the Parish Church tower in October 1937. In *Domesday Book* it was called Dunitone. Eustace, Baron of Haulton and Hereditary Constable of Chester, built a castle here – ruined in 1595. And Charles X of France stayed at Donington Park, home of the Earls of Huntingdon.

King's Mill, Castle Donington – restored beauty spot on the banks of the Trent, in August 1957.

Husbands Bosworth in April 1958. An Austin A35 pick-up truck, used for milk delivery, is on the left. The old Red Lion public house is to the right.

Cottages in Kilworth in August 1958.

North Lodge at Kirkby Mallory, pictured in April 1954. The fine old hall, which was built in Queen Anne's reign and has now been demolished, was the home of Lady Lovelace, unhappy wife of Lord Byron. From Kirkby, where she had come on a visit to her father, a few months after her marriage, she wrote to tell the poet she would never return to him. Many years later she erected a memorial arch in the grounds to their only child, Ada Augusta, who was buried with her father at Hucknall, Notts.

Looking towards Chapel Street, Syston, in January 1958.

A quiet scene in Branston-by-Belvoir in April 1957.

Subscribers

Mr R J Adams
Jean Mary Agar
Robert Ainge
David Attwood
George & Sheila Ball
Mr D J Bancroft
Christine E Barry
Rodney Bates
Geoff Bell
Bryan Blackburn
Miss M A Blow
Mrs P Bowen
Ken Brooks
Jos'e & Terry Brown and
    Maureen & Paul Walters
Peter & Brenda Brown of
    Adelaide, Australia
Steven Brown, Wigston
Mrs M Busby
Mrs S E Busby
Anne & David Carpenter
Alan Carter
Barbara Carter
Henry Thomas Causer
William G & Barbara N
    Checkland
Mrs Jean Clarke
Tom Coates
James & Debra Comery
F M Cooke
Bryan Cooper
Mrs M Crozier
J S Culpin
Marjorie Derbyshire
Michael Draycott
John & Di Driver
Ron Dyer
Marjorie & John Farmer
Anne FitzGerald
Sheila & Joe Gilford
Mr & Mrs John Glover

Christine Graham-Wilson
    (née Bell)
Anne, Paul & Natalie Harris
Trevor H Harris
A M Harrison
C D Harrison
H C Hawksworth
Ian Higgins
Tony Higgins
Walter Higgins
Mr Roy Austin Hill
Mr Terence John Hill
Mr Peter Hooke
Josephine Humberston
Robert & Anne Hutchinson
Barbara Jelley
Mr Michael Johnson
Stephen Keith Johnson
T F J Johnson
Ann, Colin, Spencer, Fraser &
    Allister Jordan
Pat & Dennis Kilsby
M E Balding & A W King
Robert A Leake
Leicestershire Archaeological
    & Historical Society
Mary & Rod Lovatt
William, Sam & George
    Loveday
Lady Martin
Mrs J A Mattock
Mrs R Mercy
Sidney Mobbs
David Mobbs
Raymond Moore
Mr & Mrs Raymond
    Murmann
R W Newcombe
David Pearson
Mr Raymond Pick
Norman Pilgrim

Ms Sharynn Porch
David Porter
Josephine Poultney
Mr Geoffrey Preston
Gillian Prince
Mrs W Pritchard
Trevor E Rands
Mrs R J Roberts
Harvey Robinson
Anthony Roe
Mr A J Sherriff
Mrs L Simmons
Neville & May Smith
Aubrey & Judith Stevenson
Dr C H Stevenson MA, BM,
    BCH(Oxon), BA, MRCGP,
    MFPHM
John William Sutton
D C & M A Tasker
Richard Taylor
Dave Tebbutt
Reginald Brian Timson
Michael Thompson
Roy Lawrence Tompkins
Dave & Delsya Turpin
In Memory of Barry Malcolm
    Ward
John Ward
Roger Ernest Ward
Michael Weston
Deryk Wheeler
John, Jennifer, Jane & Richard
    Whiston
Geoffrey L Widdowson
Mr L T Williams
Mrs Nancy Wood
Mrs M S Wright
Peter Wright & Family,
    Australia